MW00655515

The Abundant University

The Abundant University

Remaking Higher Education for a Digital World

Michael D. Smith

The MIT Press

Cambridge, Massachusetts | London, England

The MIT Press would like to thank the anonymous peer reviewers who provided comments on drafts of this book. The generous work of academic experts is essential for establishing the authority and quality of our publications. We acknowledge with gratitude the contributions of these otherwise uncredited readers.

This book was set in ITC Stone Serif Std and ITC Stone Sans Std by New Best-set Typesetters Ltd. Printed and bound in the United States of America.

Library of Congress Cataloging-in-Publication Data

Names: Smith, Michael D., 1968- author.
Title: The abundant university : remaking higher education for a
    digital world / Michael D. Smith.
Description: Cambridge, Massachusetts : The MIT Press, [2023] |
    Includes bibliographical references and index.
Identifiers: LCCN 2022059070 (print) | LCCN 2022059071 (ebook) |
    ISBN 9780262048552 (hardcover) | ISBN 9780262376358 (epub) |
    ISBN 9780262376341 (pdf)
Subjects: LCSH: Education, Higher—Effect of technological
    innovations on. | Education, Higher—Aims and objectives |
    Educational technology. | Educational equalization.
Classification: LCC LB2395.7 .S546 2023 (print) | LCC LB2395.7
    (ebook) | DDC 378.1/7344—dc23/eng/20230411
LC record available at https://lccn.loc.gov/2022059070
LC ebook record available at https://lccn.loc.gov/2022059071

10 9 8 7 6 5 4 3 2 1

Contents

Preface: Scaling the Ivory Tower

Each fall, as she has done for decades, Joyce Carol Oates teaches a creative writing seminar at Princeton University. The class is perennially popular and for good reason: Oates is one of the most beloved and accomplished writers of our age. She's written close to sixty novels and numerous collections of short stories, as well as novellas, plays, poetry, and nonfiction. She's won the National Book Award and two O. Henry Awards. She's received the National Humanities Medal. She's been nominated four times for a Pulitzer Prize. But Oates not only is a master of her craft. She also knows how to teach it expertly. She's been a professor at Princeton for more than forty years. Her Princeton colleague Edmund White calls her "Wonder Woman" for her work ethic and commitment to students,[1] and when she received professor emerita status in 2014, Princeton gave her a boxing trophy proclaiming her the "Featherweight Champion of the Literary World."[2]

Needless to say, learning from Joyce Carol Oates is a great privilege. All you have to do to get into her class is follow a few simple steps. First, get into Princeton. In 2021, the school accepted a freshman class of 1,498 students out of a pool of 37,601 applicants. That's an acceptance rate of 3.98 percent.[3] Because that rate is so low, before you apply to Princeton, you might want to boost your odds however you can—maybe by enrolling in an elite private school, paying $100,000 to hire a college admissions consultant,[4] hiring a private SAT tutor, doing volunteer "service trips" in Guatemala or Nepal, or mastering the sport of fencing. Or do them all! If you can convince somebody in your family to donate a few million dollars to Princeton, by all means, do that too.

If you're one of the lucky few who does get in, congrats: you're ready for the next step, which is to start writing tuition checks. Admittedly, this can present a challenge: these days, the full cost of attending Princeton is close to $80,000 per year.[5] The school is generous with aid, but for most students, attending involves some serious financial sacrifice.[6]

Once your tuition check clears, you can move to step three, which is to sign up for Professor Oates's creative writing seminar. To do that, you'll need to wake up by around 5:00 a.m., walk to Princeton's New South Building, and stand in a long line of other students applying for one of the ten seats in the class.[7] Regrettably, given the numbers, you might try but fail each year you're at Princeton. For the select few who do take the seminar, though, the experience is fantastic.

Until not too long ago, that was that. Only a tiny number of students had the privilege of learning from Joyce Carol Oates.

But that's changed. Professor Oates can now also be found teaching the art of short story writing for the streaming service MasterClass, which describes itself as "a world class online learning experience . . . available anytime, anywhere on your smartphone, personal computer, Apple TV and FireTV streaming media players."

MasterClass students don't get the same experience as Princeton students, of course. Professor Oates doesn't spend time with them in person, she doesn't critique their work, and they don't interact with the remarkably bright and accomplished students in her class. Still, the course is a serious and substantial one, consisting of fourteen sessions, each devoted to a different aspect of the craft. Most students who take the online course will learn a lot.

And here's the thing: the class is open to anyone who has internet access and $15 to cover the MasterClass monthly membership fee—which gives you bundled access to all sorts of other terrific professors. If writing is your thing, you can take courses taught by, among others, Margaret Atwood, Malcolm Gladwell, Salman Rushdie, and Amy Tan. Or you can branch out, studying economics with Paul Krugman, conservation with Jane Goodall, and American history with Doris Kearns Goodwin. Or how about photography with Annie Leibovitz? Journalism with Bob Woodward? Architecture with Frank Gehry?

Let me be clear: MasterClass does *not* offer students what Princeton offers, and it's not trying to. That said, there's something remarkable about the idea that an almost unlimited number of students from all over the world can take classes—whenever and wherever they want—with all of these wonderful teachers. And MasterClass has no lock on using technology to democratize access to learning. The company is simply riding a new wave of technological change that has the potential to fundamentally transform higher education.

You may already be feeling skeptical about this, especially if you work in higher education. But stay with me.

Let's pull back for a moment for some historical perspective on higher education. Over the centuries, colleges and universities have been extraordinarily stable institutions—so stable that, according to Clark Kerr, the former president of the University of California system, they comprise seventy of the eighty-five institutions in the West that have endured in recognizable form since the 1520s.[8] That's an astonishing fact. How have colleges and universities remained so stable—and, by extension, so culturally dominant—for so long?

By controlling scarce resources.

For the past five hundred years, our system of higher education has been based on a model of scarcity. In particular, it has depended on three main scarcities—of *access* (class size, selectivity), of *instruction* (faculty experts, educational support), and of *credentials* (university degrees, university reputations). These scarcities long seemed inevitable. Colleges and universities, after all, only have room in their classrooms and on their campuses for a limited number of students, so we've had to make compromises—between inclusivity and selectivity in admissions, between personalization and efficiency in instruction, between accessibility and differentiation in credentialing. These compromises are so ingrained in our educational system that today we consider it a success when a prestigious college rejects nine out of ten applicants, we take it for granted that impersonal hundred-seat lecture halls are the norm for many of our freshman students, and we shrug our shoulders when told that in 2020 our graduates carried $1.7 trillion in student loan debt—double the amount they carried just ten years earlier.[9]

By those measures, our current model of higher education is failing. Colleges and universities talk about helping students flourish in society, but tuition prices leave many students drowning in debt—or unable to enroll in the first place. We talk about creating diversity and equity on our campuses, but we rely on admissions processes that overwhelmingly favor the privileged few. We talk about preparing students for careers after graduation, but according to a 2014 Gallup survey, only 11 percent of business leaders believed "college graduates have the skills and competencies that their workplaces need."[10]

The thing is, even though we've been aware of these problems for at least half a century, we've also felt that, on the whole, the system is working. And if it's not broken, then why fix it—especially if it's lasted so long that no one can even imagine how else it might work? That way of thinking, I argue in this book, is fundamentally misguided. Our system of higher education *is* broken. In fact, it's creating all sorts of systemic injustices that make it morally and financially unsustainable, at least if you believe in the idea that affordable, high-quality higher education should be available to everybody.

That's the bad news. But there's good news too, and that's what this book is about. New digital technologies have arrived during the past decade that—if we embrace them—will allow us to create a fairer, more accessible system of higher education that, in turn, will allow us to better serve the many students who are left out of our existing scarcity-based model. These technologies can allow us to radically expand access both to the knowledge that students need to discover and develop their talents, and to the credentials that students need to signal their knowledge to employers and to use their talents to make a difference in the world.

These digital technologies have already transformed nearly every other sector of our economy, by upsetting the market power of firms and creating abundant choice, interactivity, and personalization for customers. For a long time, higher education seemed impervious to this transformation. Sure, a small number of institutions and professors dabbled in MOOCs (massive open online courses) in the 2010s, but those offerings failed to catch on and were hardly transformative within the academy. But then the pandemic hit in 2020, and almost overnight we had to integrate many new distance-learning technologies into our core degree-granting programs.

That transformation—which, on the whole, we effected remarkably quickly and successfully—showed us just how transformative new technologies can be if we choose to embrace them. If—with just a few days' notice and almost no training, and supported only by a nascent technological platform that was not designed to work at anything approaching this scale—we were able to come anywhere close to what we traditionally delivered to students in person, imagine what could be possible if universities took the time and invested the resources to embrace the full potential of digital technologies to transform our system of education.

Think about it: What if abundance could finally replace the model of scarcity that has prevailed for so long at colleges and universities? What if new technologies could allow us to understand the varied backgrounds, goals, and learning styles of our students, and could provide educational material customized to their unique needs? What if we could deliver education to students via on-demand platforms that allow them to study whenever, wherever, and whatever they desire, instead of requiring them to conform to the "broadcast" schedule of today's education model? What if the economies of scale available from digital delivery could allow us to radically lower the price of education, creating opportunities for learners we previously excluded from our finely manicured quads? Might we make room in our educational system for all sorts of talented individuals with valuable contributions to make who didn't fit within the limits of our old model? Might it now be possible, with the help of new technologies and ideas, to commit ourselves to a new system of higher education that no longer makes the rigid constraints and high cost of residential learning its centerpiece, and that instead offers students of all ages and abilities the opportunity to study and learn on their own terms?

All of that sounds dreamy, I know. And, again, I'm not saying that Berkeley, Oberlin, Princeton, Stanford, or the University of Virginia is about to disappear. Elite, traditional institutions of higher education are here to stay, and they're going to do just fine. If you have the money to pay for them, and they decide to let you in, you'll still be able to get a fantastic education from them. But in the years ahead, thanks to new technologies, the broader ecosystem that these institutions exist in is going to expand and change dramatically. Gradually, elite residential colleges and universities will lose their dominant place in that ecosystem, and customized digital learning will come to dominate a new kind of higher education—one that reaches more people and generates greater benefits for society than ever before.

*   *   *

You may well be feeling that you've heard this before. For a decade or so, we've been told that new digital technologies are going to transform higher education, but they haven't. So you can't be blamed for thinking that there's nothing special about what's happening now.

But there is. Let me explain.

I come at this topic from a unique perspective. I'm a business and management professor at Carnegie Mellon University, where I've long studied how new technologies transform industries, and time and again in my research, I've observed the same pattern. As industries of all sorts stabilize, they become overconfident, they overprice their products, and they rely on business models tailored to the physical world. This leads them to dismiss new digital technologies when they arrive, for three main reasons:

First, they don't believe that the new technologies can compete with what they're already producing. That's what happened in the music industry. "Nobody's going to listen to that shit!," one executive barked in 1997, after hearing an early demo of MP3 technology—which would soon afterward spell the end of compact discs.

Second, they don't believe they need to change because people like what they're currently paying for. That's what happened in the cable TV industry. "People will give up food and a roof over their heads before they'll give up [cable] TV," one executive said dismissively in 2013, after being asked about the threat that Netflix and other streaming services posed to cable providers.[11]

Third, they don't believe that anybody can compel them to change because they've been dominant for so long. That's what happened in the film industry. "The same six studios have dominated my industry for the last 100 years . . . and that's not going to change," a motion picture studio executive said in 2015, not long before Amazon and Netflix began producing all sorts of popular and critically acclaimed shows and movies.

Such dismissals notwithstanding, these new technologies take hold at the margins, where they create abundance in resources that were previously scarce, and gradually, this abundance allows goods and services to become more varied, customizable, and widely available. As that happens, prices fall, quality improves—and at some point, usually quite suddenly, those goods and services enter the mainstream and take over. Soon it's hard to imagine how we ever managed without them.

To many traditionalists inside of the academy, thinking about higher education from this kind of market-oriented perspective seems philosophically unpalatable. One academic recently told me, "Universities are not subject to the same market forces as profit-seeking businesses since shares are not priced and traded on public exchanges." Another opined that universities aren't businesses at all "because they have public missions and must interact with the political system."

That might sound reasonable in the faculty lounge, but it ignores a broader truth: like it or not, higher education *is* a business, at least on some levels. Students pay colleges and universities to provide them a service, after all, and students have the freedom to stop paying us if they find a better alternative to the service we offer.

As educators, we have to remember that, and we have to constantly ask ourselves how well we're serving our students. To put it in starkly commercial terms: what's our customer value proposition?

In higher education, we tend to get confused when we think about this question. Our *model* has been so stable for so long that we've conflated it with our *mission*, and we therefore see any threat to the former as a threat to the latter. No question about it, our model is under threat. As we've seen in other industries, new technologies will change how we work, and that process will hurt. But that doesn't mean we should reject those changes. Doing so would leave us saddled with our present system, which is increasingly out of date, out of touch, and—for far too many people—out of reach.

Instead, we have to focus on our core mission as educators, which to my mind is this—creating opportunities for as many students as possible to discover and develop their unique talents so they can use those talents to make a difference in the world.

It's time for us in higher education to ask ourselves some painful questions. Doesn't our decision to charge the same tuition prices and confer the same degrees for the online learning we delivered from March 2020 through September 2021 imply that online learning can be just as valuable as in-person education? And if we can do more of our teaching online, do we still need 5,000 institutions of higher learning and 800,000 professors to deliver that instruction? Does the lecture-based, "sage on a stage" model of education even work in a digital environment where data and algorithms can enable active and adaptive learning experiences? Does learning through eighty-minute lectures delivered at set times by local professors still make sense for a generation of students accustomed to consuming information on-demand from world-class talent? Is it feasible to continue charging students tens of thousands of dollars in tuition when online courses are readily available to them—courses that, once created, can be delivered to additional students with almost no additional cost? Does a college diploma have the same value in a world where employers increasingly evaluate applicants based on microcredentials and job-readiness tests instead of college transcripts, and where companies offer their own certification programs to prepare students for careers in a rapidly changing workplace?

These are difficult questions for academics to think about. So we try not to. Instinctively, it feels foolish to abandon a successful model for something untested.

*   *   *

I started to wonder about this instinctive opposition to change in early 2019. My colleagues George Chen, Pedro Ferreira, Mi Zhou, and I were trying to understand whether digital delivery could allow instructors to understand what caused students to stay engaged in their material. To do this, we partnered with Master-Class to understand how students consumed the kinds of classes I describe at the outset of this chapter—among them those delivered by not only Professor Joyce Carol Oates but also Professors Billy Collins, Roxanne Gay, Jon Kabat-Zinn, Paul Krugman, Terence Tao, Neil deGrasse Tyson, and Cornel West. MasterClass provided us with a dataset of 2.6 million anonymized viewing records for 771 MasterClass videos watched by 225,580 subscribers. My coauthors and I used machine learning techniques to characterize how instructors communicated their material—their rate of speech, their facial expressions, their tone, their hand gestures, even the number of scene changes and the color and contrast in their videos and backgrounds. We then constructed algorithms to predict how those characteristics influenced student engagement in the course material.

In 2021, we published our results in the *Journal of Marketing Research* in an article titled "Consumer Behavior in the Online Classroom: Using Video Analytics and Machine Learning to Understand the Consumption of Video Courseware."[12] In that article, we demonstrated that our machine learning framework could accurately predict how instructor delivery influenced the likelihood a viewer would continue with the course material.

The relevance of this idea to the delivery of college and university courses online seemed obvious to my coauthors and me: If we'd been able to use instructional characteristics to understand student engagement on MasterClass, shouldn't that help us understand student engagement for other higher education classes delivered online? And with enough data from different learners, couldn't we extend our models to understand the preferences of individual learners and customize our material to their individual needs?

My coauthors and I thought so. But when we presented our findings to academic seminars, conferences, and journal referees, we encountered some intense skepticism. The skeptics had no problem believing that digital tools and data analytics could be used to improve how MasterClass instructors delivered their material. But they had *lots* of trouble imagining that online teaching of any kind might actually provide a "true" education or that many people would choose it over our current model, no matter how much cheaper it was. MOOCs have been around for more than a decade, after all, and students are still lining up to pay hundreds of thousands of dollars to attend our colleges and universities. Why change?

But like it or not, change is coming, and we have a good sense of what it's going to look like. During the past quarter century, companies powered by new digital technologies have revolutionized nearly every aspect of how we live, work, and communicate. Amazon has changed how we shop. Google has changed how we search for information. Yelp and TripAdvisor have changed how we select restaurants and hotels. LinkedIn has changed how we network. Netflix, Spotify, TikTok, and YouTube have changed how we entertain ourselves. Zoom and Slack have changed how we collaborate.

A lot of us in higher education feel that we work in the one industry that's somehow different—that we're engaged in a noble mission that rises above all of this technological Sturm und Drang, that we're blessed with an age-old model that's so sacred and successful it shouldn't change. Whenever I talk about this to administrators and faculty at colleges and universities around the country, as I do often, they almost uniformly push back—sometimes dismissively and angrily—in defense of the traditional model.

I understand that reaction. Like so many others, I myself have a vested interest in preserving the status quo, which has served me very well. I received a great education from a traditional university, and I'm now in the business of delivering that same kind of education to my students. I love the academy and love being a professor. But the truth is that right now in higher education we face a far greater risk from clinging to an outmoded way of doing business than we do from changing our model to harness the potential of digital technologies.

That's why I'm writing this book. We can do better. Indeed, we have a moral *obligation* to do better. Education can do so much good for society—particularly underprivileged people in society—that we in higher education can't allow ourselves to grow complacent. Even if it's uncomfortable to do so, we must constantly be looking for ways that we can more successfully fulfill our mission as educators.

*   *   *

A good place to start, I think, is by acknowledging four fundamental truths about higher education, which I expand on in the four main sections of this book:

- First, our current system of higher education, despite its good intentions, is financially and morally unsustainable.

- Second, the problem is systemic, which means we're unlikely to solve it from within our existing scarcity-based model of higher education.

- Third, digital technologies give us an opportunity to create new systems of education based on abundance rather than scarcity—a revolutionary shift.

- Fourth, to participate in this change, those of us who work in higher education must rediscover and embrace our core mission as educators.

In recognizing these truths, we can address the main objections to change that I highlight above—that online education is inferior to residential education, that students love our high-priced product and will keep paying for it no matter how much we charge, and that new technologies will never cause a fundamental change in our system of higher education. These claims may appear superficially true, but at a deeper level, they're undeniably false. Yes, online education is worse than residential education—but only if you ignore the parts that are better. Yes, students have always paid our high prices—but that's only because they haven't had viable alternatives. Yes, new technologies haven't yet changed the business of higher education—but that doesn't mean our industry is immune to the disruptive market forces that have changed so many other sectors of the economy.

There's a lot at stake here. Soon students, employers, policymakers, and even educators will have to acknowledge that new technologies can help us deliver education that is high-quality, low-cost, widely available, and personalized in a way that classroom-bound models can't match. These changes are likely to represent a major departure from the university model as we've long known it, and that's a prospect a lot of people within higher education find both frightening and threatening. I'll admit, there are times when I feel that way myself.

But I'm also hugely optimistic about the possibilities, which in my view represent a moment of unprecedented opportunity for students, educational institutions, and society as a whole. If higher education can put its mission ahead of its prevailing model, it can embrace the changes that new technologies make possible. In doing so, it may be that we will usher in a new golden age of higher education.

But to make that possible, we first need to understand why we have such a powerful *need* for change—and to do that, we have to take a careful look at the moral and financial injustices of our current system. That's the subject of chapter 1.

I
Admissions

1

The Unjust University: Why It's Hard to Foster Inclusivity in a System Based on Exclusivity

Our system of higher education is broken.

We've known this at least since 1946, when President Harry S. Truman created a commission to explore the state of higher education in the United States. In 1947, the commission delivered a six-volume report to the president titled *Higher Education for American Democracy*. Mincing no words, the authors of the Truman Commission Report described a system that served only the well-to-do. "If college opportunities are restricted to those in the higher income brackets," they wrote, "the way is open to the creation and perpetuation of a class society which has no place in the American way of life."[1]

Stirring words. But consider this: in 2017, the Stanford economist Raj Chetty and several coauthors found that one in four children born into households in the top 1 percent of income were admitted to one of America's eighty most selective colleges and universities—compared to only one in three hundred children born into families in the bottom 20 percent.[2]

That disparity has had dire consequences. More than seventy years after the Truman Commission issued its warning, our selective institutions of higher learning are still overwhelmingly populated by students born into wealth.

Chetty and his coauthors document the wealth inequalities of who gets access to elite campuses with all sorts of sobering statistics. Thirty-eight elite colleges, including five Ivy League schools, have more students from families in the top 1 percent of the income distribution (more than $630,000 annually) than the combined number of students from families in the bottom 60 percent (less than $65,000 annually).[3] Indeed, at many elite colleges, students are more likely to find themselves sitting next to a classmate whose parents make more than $2 million annually (the top 0.1 percent of the income distribution) than a classmate whose parents make less than $25,000 annually (the bottom 20 percent).

And this wealth disparity seems to be growing. Between 2002 and 2013, the percentage of students at elite colleges who came from the top 1 percent of the income distribution increased from about 10 percent to 11.5 percent. Meanwhile, the percentage who came from families in the bottom 40 percent decreased from 10.5 percent to 8.5 percent. As a result, according to Raj Chetty's research, children born into the upper 1 percent of the income distribution are now seventy-seven times more likely to attend a highly selective college than children born into the bottom 20 percent of income.[4]

Seventy-seven times more likely.

Let that sink in. That's an appalling disparity, especially when you consider this: Chetty and his coauthors
also found that when you send poor students to the
same colleges as wealthy students, you eliminate almost
all of the lifetime earnings advantages enjoyed by the
wealthy students.

Does it have to be this way? Well, if you believe that
children born into wealth are seventy-seven times more
likely to be intellectually capable of an elite education
than children born into poverty, then, sure: our current
system of university admissions is working just the way
it should. But if you don't believe that, then you have to
conclude that something is fundamentally wrong with
how we allocate access to higher education—an institution Horace Mann referred to as "the great equalizer" of
social conditions and "the balance wheel of the social
machinery."[5] And if we're honest, it's not hard to see
what the problem is: instead of creating opportunity
and enabling social mobility, our system of higher education is perpetuating class divisions.

That's a shameful reality—a point that Siva Vaidhyanathan, a professor at the University of Virginia, made
clear in 2019 in an artfully composed tweet. Com-
menting on the charges of corruption in elite-college
admissions that emerged from the federal investigation known as Operation Varsity Blues, Vaidhyanathan
wrote, "I'm proud that when her time comes, my kid
will get admitted the old fashioned-way: by choosing

parents wealthy enough to afford a house in a good school district and an SAT prep course."[6]

Ouch.

We're most obviously perpetuating class divisions at elite colleges, but the problem extends throughout higher education. In 2016, 58 percent of children born into families in the highest income quartile earned a bachelor's degree by age twenty-four, compared to only 11 percent in the lowest income quartile.[7] And students graduating from elite universities, it turns out, have a strong advantage in the job market over graduates from second-tier universities,[8] even though there is, at best, only a weak association between the capabilities and performance of graduates from elite and less selective schools.[9]

Those sorts of advantages, not surprisingly, lead to dramatically different life outcomes. Raj Chetty and his colleagues have found that students with degrees from the Ivy-plus schools, for example, have a one-in-five chance of earning more than $630,000 by their mid-thirties, whereas students with degrees from other elite schools have a one-in-eleven chance.[10] In contrast, students with degrees from community colleges have only a one-in-three hundred chance.[11]

That's a far cry from what the authors of the Truman Commission had in mind. They looked to community colleges, in fact, as the most promising way to "remove geographic and economic barriers to educational opportunity and discover and develop individual talents at low cost and easy access."[12] And community colleges have delivered on that promise, at least in part. According to the US Department of Education, the number of students enrolled in community colleges increased from 740,000 in 1963 to 6.2 million in 2006, or about 35 percent of all students enrolled in higher education.[13]

But even if we continue to expand access to community colleges and other less selective institutions, we'll still have a problem: the degrees granted by these institutions are likely to remain significantly less valuable than the degrees granted by elite colleges. If that's the case, then elite colleges—overwhelmingly populated by children born into wealth—will continue to serve as the springboard to social mobility.

When you take all of this into account, you can't deny it: our system of higher education is fundamentally unjust. As the *Chronicle of Higher Education* observed: "American higher education has become a powerful means for perpetuating class divisions across generations."[14]

*   *   *

How did we get here? How did America's elite colleges and universities come to be populated so dominantly by children of wealth and privilege?

The problem doesn't stem from individual admissions policies or deans. It's bigger than that. It's tied to the ways our current system of higher education creates value for students and the financial costs associated with creating that value. Let's take these matters in turn.

For starters, let's state the obvious: the job market places a much higher value on degrees from elite colleges than from less selective colleges. If you want a high-paying job, where you go matters more than what you know.

What makes this disparity even more painful to confront is that poor students benefit more from attending an elite college than rich ones do. How much more? Rich students who attend an Ivy-plus college rather than no college, it turns out, are four times more likely to reach the top income quintile as an adult. That's not nothing—but poor students in that same category are *fourteen* times more likely to get there.[15]

Okay. So where you go to college strongly determines your future job-market prospects and lifetime income. That would be fine if all children had equal access to elite colleges. But they don't.

Cost is a big part of the problem. In the United States today, on average, the sticker price for a four-year undergraduate degree from a top college is close to $300,000. And since 1978, on average, tuition has risen by 1,375 percent—a rate four times greater than that of overall inflation.[16] Those are daunting numbers for almost any family to confront, especially those on the lower end of the income spectrum. According to a report by the Jack Kent Cooke Foundation, "about one in three (34 percent) of high-achieving, low-income students reported that the stated costs of tuition, fees, and room and board had discouraged them from even applying to college."[17]

Over the years, the government has tried to help. That's what Pell Grants are for. But a recent study suggests that, at least when it comes to highly selective institutions, the Pell program isn't helping. Under the Obama administration, overall funding and enrollments for Pell Grants increased dramatically, but at elite colleges, that increase apparently didn't move the admissions needle at all: between 2000 and 2013, the percentage of students in those institutions who received Pell grants remained static, at 16 percent to 17 percent.[18]

Increasingly, if you want to attend a college or university in the United States, you'll need to borrow money—lots of it—which is how we got into our current debilitating student-debt crisis. The *Wall Street Journal* summed up the situation well in 2019:

> The numbers tell the story. Borrowers currently owe more than $1.5 trillion in student loans, an average of $34,000 per person. Over two million of them have defaulted on their loans in just the past six years, and the number grows by 1,400 a day. After years of projecting big profits from student lending, the federal government now acknowledges that taxpayers stand to lose $31.5 billion on the program over the next decade, and the losses are growing rapidly.[19]

Those are terrifying numbers—again, particularly for families on the low end of the income spectrum, who, according to one recent report, annually need to finance an average amount equal to 157 percent of their income in order to send a student to college, compared to just 14 percent for high-income families.[20] For a truly astonishing picture of the extent of the problem, have a look at figure 1.1, showing that between 1989 and 2019 student loan debt for families under age 35 increased by 757 percent, a period where other forms of consumer debt barely budged.

Confronting all of this, you might think that the obvious solution would be for colleges and universities to lower their fees and then to raise them only in line with inflation. The problem is, they can't afford to.

*   *   *

Even with their current sky-high rates of tuition, elite colleges and universities consistently spend more on educating their students than they receive from them in tuition.

Caroline Hoxby has studied this topic extensively. The most selective colleges, she has found, annually spend about $100,000 per student on student-oriented services, whereas the least selective spend less than $5,000.[21] And in recent years, students at the most selective colleges have paid tuition and fees that amount to only 20 percent of what their education actually costs.

Wait—*what?* All of the tuition that these colleges receive covers only 20 percent of what they're paying to educate students? If so, how are they paying for the remaining 80 percent?

For the much of that remainder, it turns out, they're relying on a single source—gifts.[22] In effect, they're

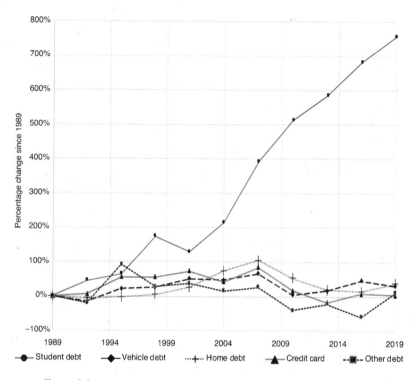

Figure 1.1

Cumulative percentage change in debts for families with heads under age thirty-five. *Sources:* Data from Federal Reserve, 2019 Survey of Consumer Finances; chart updated and adapted from Matt Bruenig, "The Median Young Family Has Nearly Zero Wealth," People's Policy Project, February 5, 2018, accessed October 27, 2022, https://www .peoplespolicyproject.org/2018/02/05/the-median-young-family-has -nearly-zero-wealth.

paying it forward, educating students at a loss today with the expectation that those students will give back lots of money tomorrow.

Of course, it might be economically rational for colleges to pay it forward to students who are likely to make big gifts down the road. The problem is that it's also economically rational for colleges to give admissions preference to students from families who are more likely to make big gifts down the road. Sadly, there is abundant evidence this is exactly what colleges and universities are doing.

For example, consider two emails that came out of the *Students for Fair Admissions v. Harvard* lawsuit. The first contains this quote from a dean to the head of admissions at Harvard:

> I am simply thrilled about all the folks you were able to admit. . . . [Redacted] has already committed to a building and . . . [redacted] committed major money for fellowships.[23]

The second contains this quote from an admissions officer explaining that a particular applicant shouldn't be included on Harvard's "clear admit" list because Harvard isn't likely to receive the family's art collection:

> Going forward, I don't see a significant opportunity for further major gifts. [Redacted] had an art collection which conceivably could come our way. More probably it will go to the [redacted] Museum.[24]

Harvard is far from the only university that takes family wealth and giving into account when making admissions decisions. For example, a 2017 article in the *Washington Post* discusses "what is regarded as an open secret in higher education: that schools do pay attention when an applicant's family has given them money—or might in the future."[25] The article then documents how the University of Virginia relies on a "VIP watch list" of wealthy donors when making admissions decisions:

> The 2011 list, for example, shows that one hopeful was initially marked as denied. Then an advancement officer scribbled a handwritten note on the tracking file: "$500k." A typed notation said "must be on WL," for wait list. A final handwritten note urged, "if at all possible A," for accepted. . . . The 2013 records show a donor's dismay after an applicant was put on the wait list. "According to people who have talked to him, [the person] is livid about the WL decision and holding future giving in the balance," an advancement officer wrote in the tracking file. "Best to resolve quickly, if possible."

*   *   *

Beyond the obvious injustice of letting family wealth influence college admissions decisions lies another troubling question: if university tuition has consistently outpaced inflation, how on earth have university *costs* consistently outpaced tuition?

A lot of this cost comes from a campus building boom. Given the lavish price of the college experience, students and parents expect the facilities to be equally lavish. Unfortunately, it costs a lot to build and maintain these facilities. As the magazine *Building Design +*

Construction put it in 2020, "In 2015, American colleges and universities went on to spend a record $11.5 billion on construction, creating 21 million [square feet] of new space even as they faced a record $30 billion shortfall in deferred maintenance costs on existing facilities."[26]

We all know what's going on. It's the edifice complex: colleges and universities are spending record amounts on new buildings because they're competing to attract the best students to their campuses with bigger and better buildings, and they're going deeply into debt to do it. Construction debt alone at some universities today has reached more than $2 billion.[27] Meanwhile, student-enrollment numbers are flat or even in decline. Writing about the situation in 2016 for *The Atlantic*, Jon Marcus quoted an official at the University of Minnesota. "It's an endless game of chasing your tail," the official said. "Every year we lose ground and costs increase."[28]

Needless to say, that means higher tuition.

But the edifice complex isn't the only reason colleges tuition has risen so much in the past twenty-five years. There's also a phenomenon that economists call Baumol's cost disease.[29]

The basic idea, which comes from a famous 1966 article by the economists William Baumol and William G. Bowen, is this: When labor productivity is rising in most of the economy, you get a problem in industries where labor productivity *isn't* rising. It's a supply-and-demand thing: in the sectors where productivity increases, labor becomes less scarce and prices fall; but as that happens, labor becomes *more* scarce and prices *rise* in the sectors where productivity *doesn't* increase. That's the origin of Baumol's so-called cost disease.

Baumol and Bowen illustrated the concept by using the example of string quartets. Even though we've seen dramatic increases in productivity in many sectors of the economy since the 1800s, nothing has changed when it comes to string quartets. To perform live today, they need the same number of musicians to put in the same amount of effort as they did two centuries ago.[30]

In terms of productivity, college professors are a lot like those violinists: we aren't any more productive today than we were in the 1800s. Our classrooms hold about the same number of students, and it still takes an hour of a professor's time to deliver an hour-long lecture to those students. In that respect, you might say, higher education is an inevitable victim of Baumol's cost disease. Because professors aren't any more productive today than they used to be, their relative cost has risen compared to other sectors, where productivity has gone up and prices have gone down. According to Baumol, who wrote about how cost disease afflicts higher education in 1967, that's why college tuitions are always on the rise:

> [T]he relatively constant productivity of college teaching leads our model to predict that rising educational costs are no temporary phenomenon— that they are not a resultant of wartime inflation which will vanish once faculty salaries are restored

to their prewar levels. Rather, it suggests that, as
productivity in the remainder of the economy
continues to increase, costs of running the educational
organizations will mount correspondingly, so that
whatever the magnitude of the funds they need today,
we can be reasonably certain that they will require
more tomorrow, and even more on the day after that.[31]

*   *   *

So here we are. And we haven't even talked about the
fact that, as the *Wall Street Journal* reported in 2019,
elite colleges use College Board data to boost their selectivity by recruiting applicants they know they won't
admit.[32] Or that for $5,000 in SAT prep classes, wealthy
parents can magically make their children 100 to 200
points "smarter" than children from families with lesser
means.[33] Or that in their competition for students,
American colleges give more aid per student to families
earning more than $100,000 per year than to families
earning less than $20,000.[34] Or that one in five high
school seniors at the Horace Mann prep school in the
Bronx (tuition price: $59,800 per year) have hired pri-
vate admissions consultants to improve their chances
of college admissions—at a time when New York City's
public schools employ one guidance counselor for every
380 students.[35]

So much for Horace Mann's 1848 vision of education
as the great equalizer of social conditions.

Everywhere you look in higher education, you find
injustices, and they're growing. The costs of higher

education are rising inexorably. The edifice complex has taken hold. So has Baumol's cost disease. Colleges and universities, paying more to educate their students than they receive in tuition, are sinking ever deeper into debt. Development officers, desperate to keep up, are chasing donors for ever larger gifts. That desperation is causing universities to make admissions decisions based on whether a student's family is likely to make big gifts. Selectivity has become a fetish, school rankings an obsession. We seem stuck with a system that, especially at the elite level, perpetuates class divisions.

I don't blame any of the actors here—not the university presidents, not the deans and the admissions staff, not the faculty, not the donors, not the parents and students. Given how the game of higher education is played, everybody is behaving in ways that make sense.

No, the real problem is bigger than the people involved. It's deeply structural, and for a long time there was nothing we could do about it.

II
Orientation

2
The Education Factory: How We Got Our Current System and Why It's Such an Expensive, Inefficient Mess

A century and a half ago, in 1872, if you were one of the roughly two hundred freshmen to enroll at Harvard College, you would have arrived for your first semester pleasantly aware that you were a member of a privileged club—one that might lead to an influential career in religion, government, or law.

You knew your education would be a traditional and relatively intimate experience. It was all laid out in the course catalog. In your first year, you and your class-mates would study the languages, literatures, and histories of ancient Greece and Rome. No young man could be considered properly educated, after all, without a background in the classics. The study of ethics was also mandatory. Under the tutelage of Andrew Preston Peabody, the Plummer professor of Christian morals who also held the title of preacher to the university, you'd study J. T. Champlin's *First Principles of Ethics* and Stephen G. Bulfinch's *Manual of the Evidences of Christianity*. You'd gain a grounding in geometry, trigonometry, algebra, and inorganic chemistry, too. And, in a concession to the modern educational fashion, you'd receive two hours a week of instruction in German grammar.[1]

Needless to say, at the national level there wasn't a huge demand for this kind of education, which was a small-scale enterprise well into the nineteenth century. Between 1810 to 1850, for example, only about sixty students graduated from Harvard each year.[2] The numbers remained low even after the Civil War. When the federal government began collecting education data, in 1870, the United States had only 563 institutions of higher learning. A total of 63,000 students were enrolled in these institutions—a figure that represented only 1 percent of the eighteen-to-twenty-four-year-old population.[3] If you do the math, you'll find that the average enrollment in American colleges was only 112 students. By today's standards, that's laughably small.

But things began to change in the latter half of the century. As industrialization came to the United States, demand grew for a more practical and widely available kind of higher education that could support a booming economy increasingly based on new technologies. The country needed highly trained agricultural scientists who could think about farming at a previously unimaginable scale and degree of specialization, and it needed young men trained in the "mechanic arts" (what today we call engineering) who could do the same for building.

On that front, Peabody and his ilk had little to offer. So in 1862, the government passed the Morrill Land-Grant Act, which set aside public land for a new kind of university—one that would "teach such branches of learning as are related to agriculture and the mechanic arts, in such manner as the legislatures of the States may respectively prescribe, in order to promote the liberal and practical education of the industrial classes in the several pursuits and professions in life."[4]

By the turn of the century, growing numbers of Americans were also seeking work in urban professions and the natural sciences,[5] fields that demanded new levels of literacy, kinds of training, and even graduate degrees. Institutions of higher learning scrambled to meet these new demands. Early in the twentieth century, Harvard had a lecture class of 520 students, which made it almost as big as Harvard's entire student body had been in 1872.[6]

But these efforts were far from systematic, and by 1916, the inefficiencies of higher education as it grew were seriously vexing a professor of education at Stanford—the gloriously named Elwood Patterson Cubberly.

Cubberly was no slouch. He became a professor at Stanford's school of education in 1906 and in the following year was appointed its dean. He received a PhD in education from Columbia University, where he had studied with, among others, John Dewey. He was the superintendent of schools in San Diego from 1896 to 1898 and served as the president of Vincennes University in Indiana from 1891 to 1896. It's fair to say he knew as much as just about anybody about America's system of higher education.

Writing that year in a book titled *Public School Administration*, Cubberly declared that to improve their system of higher education, Americans needed to look to "the lesson of the business world, from which we have much to learn."[7] If Americans wanted to meet the rapidly growing demands of the modern age, he argued, they were going to have to solve the problem of inefficiency—or, as he called it, "the large present waste in manufacture." It was time to approach higher education as a challenge of mass production.

This wasn't a new idea. More than a century earlier, Immanuel Kant, in *The Conflict of the Faculties*, had suggested that for universities "it was not a bad idea to handle the entire content of learning by mass production."[8] This idea, which led naturally to the ideas of specialization and the division of labor among faculty, took hold in the early nineteenth century and led to the rise of a German university system that powerfully influenced American educators of the period.

Chief among those American educators was the reformer Horace Mann, who in the middle of the century had successfully helped develop a new American system of public education. Cubberly himself drew inspiration from Mann. "No one did more than he," Cubberly wrote in 1919, "to establish in the minds of the American people the conception that education should be universal, non-sectarian, free, and that its aims should be social efficiency, civic virtue, and character, rather than mere learning or the advancement of sectarian ends."[9]

Social efficiency instead of mere learning—such was the new educational spirit that Cubberly hoped to inspire Americans to embrace. The work, he wrote, is "of a type with which schoolmasters are as yet but little familiar, but it is work of great future importance, work which will professionalize teaching and supervision."[10]

Cubberly then laid out thoughts that are worth quoting at some length because they capture the ethos that would come to dominate higher education in the United States in the decades to come:

> Every manufacturing establishment that turns out a standard product or series of products of any kind maintains a force of efficiency experts to study methods of procedure and to measure and test the output of its works. Such men ultimately bring the manufacturing establishment large returns, by introducing improvements in processes and procedure, and in training the workmen to produce a larger and a better output. Our schools are, in a sense, factories in which the raw products (children) are to be shaped and fashioned into products to meet the various demands of life. The specifications for manufacturing come from the demands of twentieth-century civilization, and it is the business of the school to build its pupils according to the specifications laid down. This demands good tools, specialized machinery, continuous measurement of production to see if it is according to specifications, the elimination of waste in manufacture, and a large variety in the output.[11]

And so it was—to oversimply greatly—that our educational system was transformed into something that looked a lot like a factory assembly line.

*   *   *

Cubberly wasn't the only one thinking along these lines. Notably, there was also the engineer Morris Llewellyn Cooke, who, in 1910, at the encouragement of the Carnegie Foundation, produced an influential report titled *Academic and Industrial Efficiency*.[12]

Cooke is better known today for having presided in the 1930s over the Rural Electrification Administration. But early in the century, he was known as a leading proponent of the theory of scientific management, which is why the Carnegie Foundation sought him out.

Cooke's report began with a preface by the Carnegie Foundation's president, Henry S. Pritchett, who noted that colleges and universities had recently "expanded enormously" and were now undertaking "operations of far greater complexity" than ever before. This, he suggested, presented novel management challenges that American educators were not fully equipped to cope with, hence the reason for a report from Cooke, whom Pritchett described as an expert in "the study of the efficiency of industrial establishments."

From his studies, Cooke knew that if a factory wanted to mass-produce a uniform product efficiently, it had to start with uniform raw materials. And then, using uniform processes and sets of specifications, it had to create uniformly good products—over and over and over. Any variation or imperfection on the assembly line became the enemy of efficiency. Standardization was the name of the game, and Cooke felt its time had now come in higher education.

Just a year earlier, as it happened, the Carnegie Foundation had won acceptance for a standard educational unit of measurement—one that secondary schools could use to report the amount of education they were delivering to their students. This was the so-called Carnegie unit, which is still with us today. The idea was simple: no matter where students went to school, they would now receive a standard number of these units in each of their major subjects, which would signal to the world that they had received a sufficient amount of instruction. The number of units the Carnegie Foundation proposed as sufficient in any given subject was 120—a number they arrived at by multiplying one hour a day by five days a week by twenty-four weeks a year.

Cooke recognized the value that such a system of measurement could have in the new factory model of higher education. To start, it would give colleges and universities a way of standardizing their input: they would now accept only students who had received the required number of units of secondary school instruction. But Cooke recognized that colleges and universities could also use it to measure the instruction they gave their students, which would then allow them to standardize their output. For this purpose, he called it the "student-hour," defining it as "one hour of lectures, of lab work, or recitation room work, for a single pupil." Today we know it as the credit hour.

As the factory model gained sway in the early twentieth century, colleges and universities had to concern themselves more and more with evaluating the students in their applicant pool. They looked at not only the number of credit hours high school students completed but also their grades. But how standard were those grades, *really*? Did A's in English or math mean the same thing when awarded by, say, a tiny public school in rural Texas, a big public school in Detroit, or a wealthy prep school in Massachusetts? For that matter, did a single credit hour in those places mean the same thing? Surely not. So wouldn't it be better—more efficient, more reliable—to add to the mix a single standardized test that measured every student's natural ability?

Once you make the shift to a factory model of education, with its demand for standardized inputs, such an idea is almost inevitable. Which is why, in 1926, as the number of students applying to American colleges and universities began to grow, the Scholastic Aptitude Test (SAT) came into being, created to help institutions of higher learning ensure that the raw material they were taking in each year—their students—consistently met their quality standards. The American College Testing (ACT) test got into the game as a competitor to the SAT in 1959.

And what of outputs? Student credit hours and grades were certainly helpful in measuring them because they ensured minimum standards. But what if you were an employer trying to hire students who had the same

grades and number of credit hours—but who had graduated from different institutions? How could you dif-
ferentiate them precisely in the labor marketplace? By
factoring in the value of institutional brand, which
required its own kind of standardized measurement—in
other words, a ranking system.

This idea, too, was almost inevitable once the factory
model was adopted. In fact, as early as 1910, the same
year that Cooke published *Academic and Industrial Efficiency*, the editors of *American Men of Science* published
the first ranking of American universities, based on the
number of prominent scientists associated with the institution. (Chicago, Columbia, Harvard, Johns Hopkins,
and Yale made up the top five.) In the decades that followed, as the factory model took hold, a variety of similar ranking systems came into being, among them those
created by the North Central Association of Schools and
Colleges (1924), the *American Journal of Sociology* (1931),
and the American Council of Education (1934).[13]

Let's recap here for a moment. At the beginning of
the twentieth century, facing a growing demand for
higher education (and different kinds of higher education), American educators realized that their old model
simply wasn't going to scale. So they began looking for
a different model and soon embraced what seemed the
best available option at the time—the factory assembly
line. The choice was not an unreasonable one, given that
in the business world the assembly line was enabling
a revolution of mass production. To work efficiently

in higher education, this new model demanded new input and output measurements. Again, not unreasonably, this led to the creation of standardized testing and institutional rankings. By the 1930s, everything was in place—and when the GI Bill was introduced in 1944 for veterans of World War II, the era of mass production in American higher education truly began.

The numbers tell the story. As you can see in figure 2.1, the number of students enrolled in two- or four-year degree programs in American colleges grew

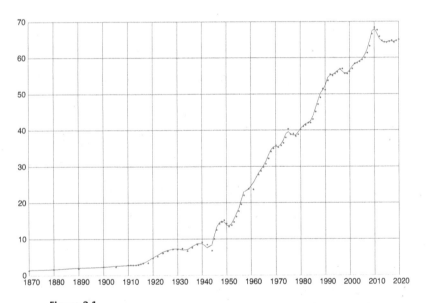

Figure 2.1
US college enrollment as a proportion of the eighteen- to twenty-four-year-old population. *Source:* Author's calculations based on data from the U.S. Census and the National Center for Education Statistics, 2021.

steadily from 1870 into the early twentieth century—and exploded after the introduction of the GI Bill. In 1870, the total number of students enrolled in college represented just 1 percent of the number of eighteen- to twenty-four-year-olds in the United States. In 2020, the ratio was 65 percent.[14]

All of that explosive growth since the 1950s has required colleges and universities to leverage economies of scale in instruction, which has led to a separation between the research and teaching functions of professors, a model of instruction through large lecture-based classes, and, from an operations perspective, the processing of students as raw inputs and standardized outputs rather than apprentices in the scholarly enterprise—all of which have given rise to what has been called "the impersonality of the multiversity."[15]

It's also meant—again, almost inevitably—that the metrics we've used to manage efficiency in our system of higher education have developed an extraordinarily outsized influence—one that, as we'll see, has been a major factor in creating the inequities and injustices that we're now saddled with.

On the input side, consider the society-shaping number of students who now take standardized tests. According to the College Board (a nonprofit organization with over $1 billion in revenue in 2017),[16] 2.2 million students took the three-hour SAT test in 2019.[17] Similarly, according to the ACT (a nonprofit organization with $350 million in 2017 revenue),[18] 1.8 million students took the three-hour-and-twenty-minute ACT test in 2019.[19] The mere act of taking these tests costs students lots of time and money, but they also spend countless hours and over $1 billion annually[20] preparing for these tests—tests which do next to nothing to make students better prepared for college.

And on the output side, consider the wildly influential rankings published each year by *U.S. News & World Report*. The magazine began publishing its rankings in 1983. Its criteria for measurement have evolved over the years, but today the ranking criteria reward colleges for increasing their "average spending per student"; for increasing the average salaries they pay to full-time assistant, associate, and full professors; and for increasing "student selectivity," determined in large degree by the average SAT/ACT scores of a college's incoming class.[21]

Are these the best measures to rank our remarkably diverse colleges and universities—and, by extension, to evaluate the remarkably diverse students who graduate from them? Almost surely not. Plenty of people are outspokenly opposed to the rankings, arguing that they perversely skew incentives and have contributed greatly to the many injustices of our present system. Nonetheless, the rankings have become such a factor in American higher education in recent years that, like them or not, everybody has to pay attention to them. The system has become a monster—one that *U.S. News* itself has described as "the 800-pound gorilla of American higher education."[22]

*   *   *

So here we are, well into the twenty-first century, locked into an assembly-line model of higher education that for decades—despite the best of intentions—has been creating, perpetuating, and amplifying social inequities.

You can't blame our colleges and universities for what's happened. Nor can you blame the SAT, the ACT, or *U.S. News*. As I've tried to make clear in this chapter, what we're dealing with is a systemic problem. The inequities that characterize our present system of higher education are the inevitable results of our assembly-line model of education, with its focus on efficiency, standardization, and the ever-more-precise measurement of inputs and outputs. For the assembly-line system to work, we need a way to rank order the quality of our inputs, and if we didn't rely on SAT or ACT scores, we'd surely rely on some other measure. Likewise, in the assembly-line model, we need a way of branding the quality of our output, and if *U.S. News* didn't provide such a system, somebody else would.

But although our system is deeply problematic today, when we adopted it, more than a century ago, we were struggling to figure out how to deliver higher education at a scale far greater than had ever been tried before. And the assembly-line model was the best available option. On a lot of levels, in fact, it has worked extremely well—just not *equally* well for everybody.

The system's failures have been apparent for a very long time. They're what animated the Truman

Commission Report back in 1946, after all. Not only that, the fixes have been apparent for a long time, too. Colleges and universities need to deemphasize admissions criteria that are heavily influenced by wealth (SAT scores, legacy status, family giving); they need to lower their costs and their tuition prices to help students from disadvantaged backgrounds gain admission and succeed in their studies; and they need to shift the focus of higher education from elitism to inclusivity.

If we know all of that, why haven't we done more to bring about change?

To answer that question, let's consider the plight of a socially minded university president who wants to make her institution more accessible to high-achieving, low-income students. One step she might very reasonably consider taking would be to decrease her school's reliance on standardized tests, which, as we've seen, strongly favor the wealthy.

That's exactly what Mark Becker did at Georgia State University. Soon after becoming the university's president in 2009, Becker worked with Tim Renick, Georgia State's chief enrollment officer, to deemphasize the SAT in the school's admissions process. The decision was based on Renick's data showing that high school grades were a much stronger predictor of college success than SAT scores, which merely predicted parental education and wealth.[23]

On many dimensions, Georgia State's move to deemphasize SAT scores in admissions has been a terrific success: the percentage of the university's students who are low-income enough to be eligible for Pell Grants has increased from 32 percent to 60 percent.[24] Today the university enrolls more students on Pell Grants than any other public research university—and three times more than the eight universities in the Ivy League *combined*.[25]

Good news, right?

Absolutely. But there was a problem. Because Georgia State deemphasized the SAT in its admissions process, by 2016, its average student SAT score had dropped by 33 points. That hurt the school's performance in *U.S. News*'s "student selectivity" category, which, in turn, caused the university to drop by thirty places in the 2016 rankings.[26]

The irony here hurts. Georgia State did the right thing to make itself a more inclusive and equitable place, and was punished for its efforts. And it's not alone. When other schools around the country have made changes that allow them to admit more students from disadvantaged backgrounds, they've paid a similar price[27]—as would our hypothetical university president if she chose to follow suit.

Now let's consider what might happen if our university president eliminated admissions preferences for children of major donors. When I floated this idea to a major donor at an elite university, he told me, "Any university who does that better not tell their donors," and noted that he would stop making donations to his university if he knew his tax-deductible "gifts" wouldn't enhance his children's admissions prospects. Surely our hypothetical university president would have had similar conversations with her major donors—and would be acutely aware that donations cover around 80 percent of the cost of educating students at her institution.[28]

But maybe she could cut costs to reduce her school's reliance on gifts? That's a great idea, in principle—but, as our hypothetical president would know, in practice, it would never work. That's because spending per student and average faculty salaries are important metrics in national rankings, which, in effect, reward colleges and universities for increasing costs, not reducing them. As William Kirwan, a former chancellor of the University of Maryland system, has observed, "If you could deliver the same quality at a lower cost, you'd go down in the rankings."[29]

Okay, it's hard to cut costs. But what about allocating financial aid more equitably? Universities typically provide more financial aid per student to families making more than $100,000 per year than to families making less than $20,000 per year.[30] What if they were to give more of that money to high-performing students with the greatest financial need? Also a nonstarter, as our president would know all too well. Shifting financial aid away from wealthy families would almost certainly hurt future giving to the university. "Enrollment managers know there is no shortage of deserving low-income students applying to good colleges," the education reporter

Paul Tough wrote in the *New York Times* in 2019. So why don't colleges accept more of these students? "Because," Tough says, "they can't afford to."[31]

The lesson here is simple: it's hard to change a system from the inside. For a long time in higher education, that's just been the way it is. There really isn't much even a hypothetical university president with the best of intentions can do. So we've swallowed our distaste for the system's inequities and have just carried on. But now, with the advent of the internet and new digital technologies, outside forces are opening up real possibilities for change.

But to identify and to take advantage of those possibilities, we first have to understand more precisely how our current factory system has been holding us back. The key idea to grasp here is that any factory system involves three main functions: it selects raw materials, processes them, and delivers them to the market. In our system of higher education, that translates to admitting, educating, and credentialing students. And here's what really matters. At any college or university, each of these three functions is based on the allocation of scarce resources, which, in turn, represent the source of the institution's market power.

In the following three chapters, we'll take a close look at those scarcities—each of which has long held us captive in higher education but, at last, no longer needs to.

3

Seating Arrangements: Why Limited Classroom Space Leads Rich Parents to Bribe Their Kids into College

On March 12, 2019—as part of Operation Varsity Blues, a wide-ranging investigation by the Department of Justice into corruption in college admissions—federal prosecutors issued indictments against an educational consultant named William Singer.

At the time, Singer served as the head of two nonprofit organizations, the Key Worldwide Foundation and the Edge College & Career Network. Prosecutors presented evidence that thirty-three parents paid over $25 million in bribes to these organizations, which then bribed test proctors to change answers on the donors' children's SAT tests and college coaches to recommend their children as prized recruits in sports they had never played. Singer has subsequently admitted to providing unethical college admissions services to more than 750 families.[1] In a call tapped and recorded by the investigators, he told one prospective client, "What we do is we help the wealthiest families in the U.S. get their kids into school."[2]

Plenty of legitimate independent educational consultants have made that their goal, too. Business is booming for them. The Independent Educational Consultants Association, a trade organization for college counselors, estimates that the number of independent educational consultants has tripled in the last five years. It also cites a survey saying that 26 percent of students seeking a four-year college degree used an independent educational consultant during that period, up from only 3 percent ten years ago.[3]

Those services don't come cheap. A low-end counselor might charge $200 to $300 an hour, but the sought-after ones can charge between $500 and $1,500 an hour. Or they sell whole "packages." Allen Koh, the CEO of Cardinal Education, a San Francisco Bay Area college counseling firm, explained to the *Wall Street Journal* what his firm charges for that comprehensive kind of treatment. "Our most common package is about $50,000," he said. "Our most expensive package is $350,000, and then there are some special cases for which we're charging a million, sometimes even more."[4]

There's clearly lots of money to be made in this business. One estimate puts its market value at some $2 billion.[5] But that raises an important question: why on earth are parents willing to shell out so much money— and, in the case of Singer's clients, risk jail time—to get their kids into college? There are some 4,500 colleges and universities in the United States, after all, and those schools collectively have plenty of room to accommodate our current pool of prospective students.

The answer, naturally, has to do with scarcity. The families who work with expensive educational consultants aren't interested in getting their kids into just any school. They want admission to the most selective ones—and those aren't abundant. According to *U.S. News*, only twenty-three colleges and universities in the United States accept fewer than 10 percent of their applicants.[6] Together, these twenty-three schools represent a small fraction of the country's total number of colleges and universities, but they hold a disproportionate amount of the power and influence in higher education. Why? Because, individually, each of them controls an important scarce resource—*access*.

*   *   *

Not everybody buys in to the idea that you have to go to a selective school. A common refrain is that people who want to go to college in this country have all sorts of terrific options available to them, so they should stop being so uptight about getting in to the "best" one possible.

The Netflix documentary *Operation Varsity Blues: The College Admissions Scandal*, showcased this point of view. "You have infinite choices," Akil Bello, a test-prep expert, told the filmmakers. "Forget about USC. Go someplace else." The filmmakers also talked to Barbara Kalmus, an independent education consultant, who made a similar point. "What are we doing to these kids," she asked, "by pounding them into the ground with 'Top 25, Top 10, Top 5'? Because, ultimately, where you do go to school has little or no effect on what will happen to you in the future."

That sounds egalitarian and sensible, right? "Chill out, people: it's all going to work out just fine." There's only one problem: that's just not true.

Like it or not, where you go to college has an enormous influence on your future career options and career earnings. Consider the findings of Thomas R. Dye, a professor of political science at Florida State University. In the eighth edition of his book *Who's Running America?*, Dye found that half of our nation's top business and government leaders graduated from just twelve universities. That's an astonishing concentration of power in the hands of just a few institutions, right? But what's more astonishing is this: one in five of our nation's elite leaders graduated from Harvard University.[7]

But correlation isn't causation. Maybe these leaders would have done just as well in their careers if they had graduated from less prestigious colleges. One way to determine causality between college admissions and job-market outcomes would be to randomly assign students to less or more selective schools and then to observe the difference in salaries between the two groups. That sort of experiment is nearly impossible to execute, but in the mid-2000s, Mark Hoekstra obtained a data set that allowed him to approximate it. The data set consisted of two groups of students—one in which everybody had been barely accepted by a state's flagship university and the other in which they had all been barely rejected. Those who were just barely accepted had basically the same qualifications as those who were just barely rejected, which meant that any difference in wages between the two groups could be attributed to the school's admissions decision rather than the inherent quality of the applicants.

Hoekstra published the results of his study in 2009 in the prestigious *Review of Economics and Statistics*.[8] His findings were revealing: ten to fifteen years after graduating, the students who had been barely admitted to the flagship university were making approximately 20 percent more than the students who had been barely rejected by the flagship university. A 20 percent wage premium in that amount of time is a big deal—big enough, in fact, that you'd be making a perfectly rational economic decision if you decided to shell out lots of money to buy your eighteen-year-old one of the scarce seats at a highly selective college or university.

*   *   *

But there are two sides of this equation. We've seen that students and parents are doing whatever they can to get access to classroom seats at selective institutions. But those institutions themselves—however devoted they might appear to be to the goals of diversity and inclusivity—are also doing whatever they can to make their seats appear as scarce as possible.

My family, like lots of others, has been affected by this phenomenon. Shortly after our sons took the practice SAT test, they were deluged by letters of interest from colleges that told them how much they hoped they would apply. Some of these colleges even offered to waive their application fee, simply because our kids seem to be such a good fit.

This seemed only natural to my wife and me. What college *wouldn't* want to recruit our bright and talented sons? But the more these letters came in, the more we started to wonder what was going on. Many of them, we realized, came from schools where our sons had very little realistic chance of gaining admission.

As we talked to other parents of students who were starting to consider colleges, we heard similar stories: their kids, too, were being invited to apply to elite schools that, at least on paper, they had very little chance of getting in to. A November 2019 article in the *Wall Street Journal* confirmed our anecdotal observations: the article reported that a number of schools were indeed buying student data from the College Board and using that data to recruit students that they knew they wouldn't admit.[9]

Why would they do that? Simple. The more students a school rejects, the more it appears to control a scarce resource—a very limited number of highly desirable classroom seats. And the scarcer their admissions opportunities, the more prestigious and powerful they become. The education writer and college administrator

Matt Reed described the situation memorably when recounting a conversation with his daughter about why she was being recruited by a highly selective school. "They want you to apply so they can reject you," he wrote on the website *Inside Higher Ed*, "and brag about how hard it is to get in."[10]

That seems to be what has been happening at the University of Chicago, which repeatedly sent letters of interest to one of our sons. In 2006, Chicago had a 44 percent undergraduate acceptance rate, a number that was causing it to lag behind many of its peers in the *U.S. News* rankings. To fix that "problem," the school bought student-level SAT scores and contact information from the College Board, and then used that data to recruit students it knew it wouldn't admit.[11] The strategy worked like a charm. In the years that followed, Chicago steadily reduced its admit rate, reaching 27 percent in 2009, 8.8 percent in 2016, and 5.9 percent in 2019.[12] And guess what? During that same period, the school rose in the *U.S. News* rankings from fifteenth[13] to fourth.[14]

Because it's so easy to boost selectivity in this way, a lot of schools are getting into the game, as that *Wall Street Journal* report made clear. At times, they're even doing this in a way that seems cynically exploitative of minority students. A recent National Bureau of Economic Research paper determined that Harvard, for example, may have been doing just that. "Harvard encourages applications from many students who effectively have no chance of being admitted," the authors of the report wrote, adding, "This is particularly true for African Americans. African American applications soared beginning with the Class of 2009, with the increase driven by those with lower SAT scores. Yet there was little change in the share of admits who were African American."[15]

*   *   *

Recruiting students that you know you won't admit is only one way to make admissions opportunities artificially scarce. Another is to simply reduce the number of students you admit. That's exactly what George Washington University did in 2019. After noting that its selectivity had slipped over the previous five years,[16] the university announced that it would reduce its enrollment by 20 percent[17]—despite at the time having what the *Washington Post* described as "growing enrollment, solid finances, expanding research prowess and robust demand for programs such as politics and international affairs." GW's president explained the decision openly to the *Post* as a play for exclusivity. "Harvard's in the quality business," he said. "They're not in the quantity business. GW should be in the quality business, too."

Reacting against this drive for exclusivity, outside observers have recently started to argue, idealistically, that elite schools need to move in the opposite direction and radically *expand* the number of students they admit. All sorts of people have made this argument.

"Selective colleges could substantially increase the size of their undergraduate populations," wrote the authors of an April 2021 report titled "Innovation and Justice: Reinventing Selective Colleges" produced by Harvard's Graduate School of Education, "creating exciting, rigorous pathways to bachelor's degrees that are more accessible, appealing, and affordable for a greater diversity of students."[18] Writing in an April 2021 *Washington Post* editorial, the journalist and higher education author Jeff Selingo argued that "the ever-declining proportion of applicants accepted at . . . top-ranked universities should spur them to consider making their freshman classes substantially larger."[19] And in the May 2021 issue of *The Atlantic*, the Yale Law School professor Daniel Markovits proposed that the government should get involved by requiring exclusive universities to "double or even triple their enrollments" or risk losing their tax exempt status.[20]

Colleges and universities have a standard response to this kind of suggestion. Nice idea, they say, but let's get real: the only viable way to deliver a high-quality education is in person and on campus, with professors and students doing their work together in classrooms that have a limited number of seats.

When we adopted the factory model for higher education early in the twentieth century, that argument was unassailable. We simply didn't have the technological capability to deliver a high-quality education remotely. But that's no longer the case—as the National

Education Equity Lab, a nonprofit organization, demonstrated recently when it enrolled hundreds of high school juniors and seniors from high-poverty schools in an online Harvard literature class. As Jeff Selingo noted in the *Washington Post* op-ed cited above, this class had "the same assignments and standards as its equivalent" on the Harvard campus. Of those who enrolled in the class, 90 percent were students of color, 89 percent passed, and almost two-thirds received A's or B's, prompting the University of California Berkeley professor David Kirp to write in the *New York Times*: "Although the students who earned those A's and B's would probably flourish at an Ivy League school, few of them will get the chance."[21]

There's another recent experiment that has demonstrated that we can deliver high-quality education at a distance to a lot of students—the experiment with remote learning that we've just conducted during our pandemic year. There were hiccups as we adapted, but teaching by Zoom worked surprisingly well. Our colleges and universities seem to agree that distance education can deliver as much value as on-campus education. After all, they didn't lower their tuition prices when they made the switch—and they wouldn't knowingly overcharge students for an inferior product, would they?[22]

*   *   *

If we want to make our system of higher education more equitable and just, the right thing to do would be to expand the number of opportunities for students to study at elite colleges. This is especially true now that we have evidence that they can do this without sacrificing the quality of the education they provide. But the regrettable fact is that's never going to happen, at least within our existing system of scarcity-based education.

In his *Atlantic* article, Markovits correctly observes that by doubling or tripling their enrollment, selective universities "would immediately dampen admissions and rankings competition and soon, by increasing the supply of graduates, reduce the competitive value of 'elite' degrees." Sounds reasonable. But here's the problem. Reducing the competitive value of elite degrees might be beneficial from a social perspective, but administrators at elite schools aren't paid to operate from a social perspective. They're paid to serve and protect the interests of their institutions, and in our current system the best way for them to do that is to continue to pursue exclusivity, regardless of its cost to society.

As I've said before, I don't blame them for this. Like the wealthy parents who use bribes to get their kids into selective colleges, college administrators who do their best to make their institution artificially selective are simply playing the game by the rules they've been given. The same principle is at work in both of those cases: people tend to act in their own self-interest, and it's hard to get them to act against it. But that's exactly what we're doing when we ask wealthy parents not to use their resources to enhance their kids' prospects, or when we ask college administrators to make decisions that go against the competitive interests of their institutions.

One way to change the incentives of parents and administrators is by prosecuting people who break the law, which is what the Department of Justice did when it prosecuted William Singer and his wealthy clients. Another way is to write new laws, which is what Daniel Markovits was proposing when he suggested that we put institutions' tax-exempt status at risk if they don't admit more students.

Both of those approaches take our current system of higher education for granted and just tinker with it at the margins. There's nothing wrong with doing that. But, as I've been arguing, that approach is unlikely to bring lasting justice and equity into higher education, given the nature of our factory model. So we need to think more creatively, ambitiously, and expansively. How might we change the whole system?

More than a century ago, as is discussed in chapter 2, we made a reasonable decision to adopt a factory assembly-line model of higher education where the factory had three main roles—selecting raw materials, processing those raw materials, and bringing the finished products to market. Over time, that system has inevitably created a set of perverse parental and institutional incentives in how we assign students to our scarce classroom seats. As we've seen, that, in turn, has led to outcomes that are painfully unequal and unjust.

No matter how many universities exist across the market for higher education, if there's local scarcity in the number of students who can be admitted to any individual institution—which is very much the situation at our selective schools today—then each institution faces an optimization problem and naturally will try to admit the "best" students it can find.

With perfect foresight, the right way to define "best" is based on outcomes: which students are going to complete their degrees and make the best use of their education in their careers and in society?

The problem is, there's no easy way to predict student outcomes at the time schools make their admissions decisions. How can you predict which seventeen-year-olds in your applicant pool are most likely to finish their degrees and make good use of their education in society? You can't—at least, not well. So universities do the best they can by using a set of limited metrics to make up-front guesses about who will be most successful—metrics like high school grades, extracurricular activities, and standardized test scores. And, needless to say, the wealthy and the well-connected manipulate those metrics in their own favor. That's human nature.

For their part, parents and students face a similar optimization problem. At the same time institutions are trying to find the best students for their either-or admissions decisions, parents and students are trying to find the best institution for their either-or enrollment decision. That decision is based on another uncertainty:

where will they get the best return on investment for their time and tuition dollars? And today, the best way to make that decision is again to use a limited set of metrics—the *U.S. News* rankings, the likelihood that a school's alumni network and the classmates you meet in college will be able to open doors for you down the road, and the likelihood that employers will be impressed by the name brand of your institution.

In other words, in our current system, exclusivity creates demand, which is why so many of our schools are engaged in a nonstop race to become ever more selective. Just thirty years ago, no school had an admit rate lower than 17 percent, and only twenty schools had a rate below 33 percent.[23] In 2019, by contrast, fifty-seven schools had admit rates lower than 17 percent, and more than a hundred had admit rates below 33 percent.[24] In the spring of 2021, at the extreme end of the spectrum, Harvard's admit rate was 3.4 percent, Princeton's was 4 percent, and Yale's was 4.6 percent.[25]

With rates that low, *of course* anxious parents and students are going to do whatever they can to boost their odds. And to keep up, *of course* schools are going to try to juice their selectivity. That's why so many schools are now playing games—setting artificial limits on capacity, recruiting students who will never be admitted, and doing everything they can to artificially boost their rankings and their reputations.

4

Masters of None: Why We Standardize Our Teaching Even Though We Know Our Students Are Unique

In the previous chapter, we talked about the scarcity of *access* in higher education and how the escalating battle among selective institutions to control it is warping our admissions process. Admissions is the first step in the factory model of higher education in that it involves the selection of raw materials. The next step is the processing of those raw materials—educating our students. And that brings us to the second of the three scarcities on which our current system is based: *instruction*.

To begin, let's go back to 1968, when the educational psychologist Benjamin Bloom developed an instructional strategy that he called "mastery learning."[1] Bloom based his strategy on a simple idea: students learn best when they're allowed to master basic subjects before they tackle more advanced ones. Mastery learning requires educators to provide students with the time necessary to master materials at their own pace, which means that students should be treated as individuals who have unique backgrounds, learning preferences, and pedagogical needs.

But Bloom didn't propose this individualized style of learning as just a theoretical possibility. He conducted research that proves it works. Students taught using mastery learning techniques, he discovered, outperformed students trained in conventional one-size-fits-all classrooms by 400 percent. Shown graphically, this difference in performance looks a lot like the "deadweight loss" that you may have learned about in microeconomics,[2] but with an important difference. In microeconomics, deadweight loss measures the economic gains that could be realized in perfectly efficient markets. Bloom's chart measures the gains in human potential and possibilities that could be realized if we adopted more effective techniques for educating students.

Bloom hated all of the lost potential he saw in that graph. In fact, he hated the idea that instructors would assume that student performance should necessarily follow a bell curve distribution at all. Is it not absurd, he asked, that we take that kind of distribution for granted in education—that in any given class we would expect that there are a certain percentage of high achievers and a roughly equivalent percentage of low achievers? When did instructors decide that conforming student outcomes to a normal distribution represents *success*?

Bloom railed against this way of thinking. "Much of the effort of the schools and the external examining system," he wrote in his 1968 article, "is to find ways of rejecting the majority of students at various points in the education system and to discover the

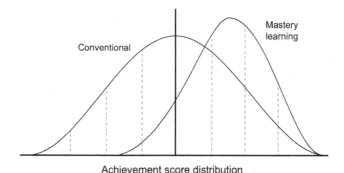

Achievement score distribution

Figure 4.1
Performance differences with mastery learning. *Source:* Adapted from James H. Block, "Introduction to *Mastery Learning: Theory and Practice*," in *Mastery Learning: Theory and Practice*, ed. James H. Block (New York: Holt, Rinehart and Winston, 1971), 7; and Benjamin S. Bloom, "The 2 Sigma Problem: The Search for Methods of Group Instruction As Effective As One-To-One Tutoring," *Educational Researcher* 13, no. 6 (1984): 5.

talented few who are to be given advanced educational opportunities."

Sound familiar?

During the past fifty years, higher education has relaxed its slavish conformity to grading based on forced curves,[3] but the concept lives on in introductory, "weed-out" courses that are designed to cull the herd of its weaker members. The former acting governor of Massachusetts and educational reformer Jane Swift summarized her concerns about such courses in an April 2021 tweet:

> Reason gazillion we don't have more STEM grads? Daughter (currently has a 4.0 in her math major) being

told Computer Science req'd course is "impossible"—
peers say avg for first exam is 15%. Isn't that an
indictment of the professor?[4]

Yes! Or at the very least, it's an indictment of the system. That's certainly what Bloom's research suggested.
In his paper, Bloom went on to talk about how mastery learning (paced instruction, personalized review)
improves student outcomes, and why it's stupid to
assume that a student who might take longer to grasp
a particular topic is—well, stupid. "If we are effective in
our instruction," he wrote, "the distribution of achievement should be very different from the normal curve,"
adding, "If the students are normally distributed with
respect to aptitude, but the kind and quality of instruction and the amount of time available for learning are
made appropriate to the characteristics and needs of
each student, the majority of students may be expected
to achieve mastery of the subject."[5] Sounds pretty reasonable to me.

Bloom continued to explore the potential of mastery
learning and in 1984 published an article in which he
discussed the advantages of combining it with one-to-
one tutoring.[6] What he found—as shown in the graph
below—is that while mastery learning on its own can
deliver a one standard deviation increase in student performance over conventional instruction, combining it
with one-on-one instruction increases the mean of student performance by two standard deviations above the
mean of conventional instruction. What this means in

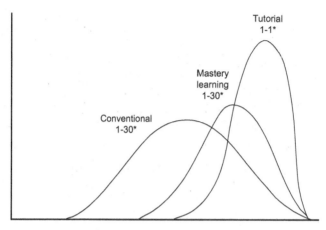

Summative achievement scores

*Teacher-student ratio

Figure 4.2
Performance differences with mastery learning and individual tutoring. *Source:* Adapted from Benjamin S. Bloom, "The 2 Sigma Problem: The Search for Methods of Group Instruction as Effective as One-to-One Tutoring," *Educational Researcher* 13, no. 6 (1984): 5.

practice is that the average student who receives a combination of mastery learning and one-on-one instruction performs better than *98 percent* of the students who receive conventional instruction.

The implications of this shift are profound. Consider a class of a hundred students. Bloom found that when the class was taught using conventional instruction, two students received an A+ and that when those same students were taught using a combination of mastery learning and one-on-one instruction, forty-eight more of them achieved A+ mastery.

All of this raises an obvious question: if mastery learning and one-on-one learning are so much better than traditional classroom instruction, why don't we use them more? The answer, unfortunately, is just as obvious: mastery learning and one-on-one learning aren't cost-efficient at scale.

In short, the problem comes back to scarcity—a scarcity of instruction that can be tailored to the individual needs of students.

*   *   *

Okay, so you've got lots of students and relatively few instructors. The instructors are the scarce resource here, and they're bound in space and time. To learn from them, you have to be on the campus *where* they teach and in the classroom *when* they teach. A single professor teaches the same content to many students from, say, 9 a.m. to 10:20 a.m. on Tuesdays and Thursdays, from early September to mid-December, in room 1206, in Hamburg Hall, on Carnegie Mellon University's campus, in Pittsburgh.

This scarcity creates two broad categories of problems—one for instructors and one for students. Let's take those in turn.

The problem for instructors, at least for those who altruistically care about the quality of their teaching (more on that in a second), is that they don't have time to give their students the individual attention that they deserve—and that mastery learning demands.

When I teach to a room of thirty students, I'm quite sure that three to five of them are bored (and could go faster) and three to five are lost (and need more time grasp the concept). The challenge is that I usually don't know which ones they are—and even if I did, I wouldn't be able to do much about it because I'm busy trying to keep the middle twenty students in the class happy and engaged.

This problem is even worse in classes where students have diverse backgrounds. One of the hardest classes to teach in the management program I'm a part of is Introduction to Accounting and Finance. Why? Because instead of just a few students in the tails of the distribution, this class typically has lots of students with strong finance backgrounds, and lots of students with no finance background. So instead of just a handful of students who are either bored or lost, introductory accounting professors know that most of their students fall into one of those two buckets—and in a single eighty-minute lecture, they just can't give each individual student what they need.

That's a problem caused by student backgrounds. There's a related problem that arises from instructor backgrounds. Like most professors, I'm regularly asked to teach topics that don't align with what I'm most qualified to teach. To achieve tenure in the academy, you have to become a world-recognized expert in a specific area of study. In my case, that meant investing a great deal of time and effort in becoming an expert in how information technology and digitization impact structure and competition in markets.

In short, the tenure process produces specialists, and that's a good thing—at least until you get into the classroom. At that point, you discover that there aren't enough people on any given college campus to make it economically efficient to deliver a fourteen-week class on, say, the strategic and economic implications of technological change in digital markets for entertainment goods. As a result, educators who are trained as specialists are forced to teach as generalists. This means we have to convey our colleagues' expertise second-hand. When I talk to students about technology and firm productivity, for example, I have to work hard to absorb and convey the work of Stanford's Erik Brynjolfsson; when I discuss innovation and crowdsourcing, I'm doing my best to relay the work of NYU's Natalia Levina; when I talk about the use of machine learning algorithms in business and social settings, I have to channel the research of Harvard Business School's Edward McFowland; and when I talk about the risks of algorithmic bias, I'm trying to understand and summarize the work of MIT's Catherine Tucker.

That's a lot of work, and sometimes it makes me feel like I'm a one-man band playing a bunch of instruments poorly instead of playing my preferred instrument well. Wouldn't it be better—for me and for my students—to cut out the middleman and allow students to learn directly from the experts on a particular topic?

But it's not that simple. Even if I were able to convince Erik and Natalia and Ed and Catherine to join the band by speaking to my class, we'd still need a conductor—someone willing and able to help everyone understand how each instructor's separate topic fits into the main goals of the class and to develop the important connections between the material that the subject expert is presenting, the material that the class has already covered, and the material that is yet to come.

Okay, so there's scarcity in access to experts on different topics. But there's also scarcity when it comes to experts who study the same topic. Consider the research that Harvard Business School professor Anita Elberse and I have conducted on the managerial implications of what's known as the Long Tail—the low-level but cumulatively significant sales of niche products that become possible when you move from physical stores with limited shelf space to digital stores with unlimited shelf space. I have a world of respect for Anita's intellect and research, but I disagree with her conclusions about the strategic importance of the Long Tail for media executives. This creates some awkwardness for me when I talk to my students because, given my biases, I feel like I give Anita's position short shrift. Wouldn't it be better if my students could hear me make the best case for my position and hear Anita make the best case for hers? Why don't we do that? Because Anita teaches in Cambridge, Massachusetts, and I teach in Pittsburgh, Pennsylvania, and for both of us, time is scarce.

Now that you know how scarcity makes my job difficult, let's spend some time looking at the problems instructional scarcity creates for students—you know, the people who are often paying $60,000 or so a year to receive an education from me and my colleagues.

Some are easy to identify. In large, impersonal lectures, students can easily become bored or lost, neither of which is optimally conducive to learning. Similarly unsatisfactory is taking classes from instructors who have to muddle through when teaching subjects that fall outside of their areas of expertise, or instructors who, consciously or unconsciously, present the ideas of others in a misleading or biased way because they disagree with them.

Then there's the role an instructor's gender and race can play in student outcomes, a burgeoning area of academic research. In a 2021 paper published in the *Journal of Marketing Research*, for example, two University of Michigan faculty members studied whether female students benefit from having female professors.[7] Specifically, they looked at the grades of undergraduate students at the business school of a public midwestern university and noticed that the grades of female students in quantitative classes were significantly lower than those of their male peers, even after controlling for the students' measured aptitudes, grade-point averages, family backgrounds, and demographic characteristics.

But here's where things get interesting: that performance gap virtually disappeared when those female students were taught by a female professor. Why? According to the authors, it's because, at least for women, instructors of the same sex "increase female students' interest and performance expectations in quantitative courses and are viewed as role models by female students." A 2010 study of the performance of male and female cadets at the US Air Force Academy came to a similar conclusion: taking a math and science class from a female professor eliminates the gender gap between male and female students in science, technology, engineering, and mathematics (STEM) classes, and significantly increases the likelihood of women graduating with a STEM degree.[8] These papers aren't saying that women in technical disciplines benefit from *always* having female instructors. Rather, these studies show that female students in subjects that have historically been dominated by men benefit from having *some* female instructors who can mentor them and give them examples of success among people who look "like me."

Other papers have found similar results for underrepresented racial and ethnic minorities. A paper published in 2014 in the *American Economic Review* titled "A Community College Instructor Like Me" noted a significant gap at community colleges between the dropout rates and grade performance of white and underrepresented minority students—and found that the gap closed by as much as 50 percent when classes were taught by instructors who themselves were from an underrepresented group.[9] I could cite other studies, but I suspect you get the idea: underrepresented students do better when they are able to identify with the person who is teaching them. The problem underrepresented students in my class face is that my identity is fixed in such a way that I can't give them this opportunity.

Another problem students have when access to instructors is scarce is this: they have a tough time getting into classes taught by the most popular professors. At one level, this is just a numbers game: professors are paid to teach a certain number of classes per year and can accommodate only a certain number of students in those classes. But there are other factors to consider—including, perhaps not so surprisingly, faculty egos.

Not long ago, Steven Levitt, who teaches economics at the University of Chicago and is a coauthor (with Stephen Dubner) of the bestselling *Freakonomics*, told a funny story to make this point, which itself highlights a larger point: when it comes to instruction, scarcity is sometimes manufactured.[10] For years, whenever Levitt taught his popular Economics of Crime class, he had to limit it to roughly eighty students because that was the maximum capacity of the biggest lecture hall available to his department. He found that very frustrating. What if a student came to Chicago with a specific interest in this class but each year was closed out? It didn't seem fair, so Levitt finally made a bit of a stink and got access to a lecture hall that seated three hundred students, which filled up quickly. Imagine his surprise when, the following fall, he learned that he would once again be teaching his class in the smaller lecture hall.

To an economist, the decision made no sense. The demand was there, so the supply should be too. When Levitt went to his department chair to complain, the chair said, "Well, the problem is, all the other faculty members got really upset because there were hardly any students in their classes, and they complained so much that I'm going to lower you back down to eighty again." To which Levitt responded, "This is the University of Chicago Department of Economics, and our solution is to . . . not let people have what they want?"[11]

There's one more problem worth mentioning briefly: for students, scarce access to faculty creates a challenge not only when they're choosing classes but also when they're choosing which university to attend in the first place. That's because not all great professors teach at the same university. Getting into Stanford University means you *might* be able to learn from Erik Brynjolfsson—but it also means you definitely *won't* be able to learn from MIT's Catherine Tucker.

*   *   *

Universities are aware that students and parents are making college choices based in part on the faculty who teach there. Universities are also acutely aware that they can employ only a limited number of instructors, so naturally they want to hire and keep the "best" ones. That makes perfect sense: in our current model, universities maintain their institutional power by hiring and retaining the professors who are widely acknowledged to be the best.

But how do universities determine who is "best"? In the case of hiring decisions, selective universities pretty much have to focus on metrics that tell them which professors are the most likely to enhance the academic prestige of the university because prestige is an important source of their market power. In practice, this means that selective universities hire and promote tenure-track professors based not on how well they teach but on how good their CVs look.

As with the other choices we've discussed in this chapter, this creates a couple of distortions. The first has to do with institutional power. When faculty affiliation is scarce, faculty will want to align themselves with the most prestigious universities, which typically are those that already have the most prestigious faculties. This natural feedback loop makes it hard to change the established order of institutional power in the higher education market.

The other distortion has to do with the incentives this gives to tenure-track faculty. When I was finishing my PhD, a senior colleague gave me some important career advice. The only thing that matters in the tenure process, he told me, is the number of publications you have in top academic journals. If you're a truly terrible teacher, he said, it might hurt your chances of getting tenure—but moving from being a mediocre teacher to the best instructor in your department won't help your tenure chances at all, so don't spend your time working toward that goal. Instead, figure out how much time it takes for you to get ranked as an average teacher in your department, and put in no more time than that. If, for example, you find you need to prep for an hour to teach classes that students rank as average, then start preparing for class about an hour before class starts. That way you'll never waste time on teaching.

I had a hard time putting that into practice. The embarrassing truth is that I love teaching, and I believe that being a good teacher is an important way to serve my students. I knew it wouldn't help me get tenure, but it seemed like the right thing to do. Before getting tenure, I even managed to win our school's annual award for excellence in teaching. This, however, turned out to be a misstep. "Clearly," one influential professor at another university told me, "you're spending too much time on your teaching and not enough on your research." Up to that point, I'd believed being a good teacher would have no effect on my tenure prospects. But my colleague was gently informing me that, at least at research institutions, being celebrated as a great teacher could actually hurt my career by signaling that I wasn't a serious scholar.

For a long time, I didn't pay much attention to this distortion. I was able to earn tenure at a top research institution by doing the research I love while still delivering the quality instruction my students deserved. No problem, right?

I felt that way right up until my oldest son started college and announced that he was taking an introductory class in microeconomics. "Great," I said. "You'll love it. It's all about consumer behavior, firm behavior, strategy, incentives, and making money."

But here's the problem: the class was taught by a professor who was too busy with his research to give individual grading feedback to a class of thirty students. This professor seemed to be doing just barely enough to be an average teacher, and was perfectly content with a room full of students who were, bored, lost, or—as in the case of my son—both.

I don't know that I blame that professor. He was doing exactly what his incentives told him to do. He was an economics professor, after all. I'm also not sure I blame the promotion and tenure committees at research universities across the country for allowing this to happen. They, too, are simply following their incentives. They compete in a market where students are drawn to schools with strong reputations, and where those reputations are determined by surveys of faculty who care a lot more about a school's research quality than its teaching quality.

What concerns me is how we allocate scarce teaching resources in our current system of higher education. Does it make sense to ask professors to become experts in niche areas of research and then share their expertise only with the small number of students on any given campus who might care about that niche subject? Does it make sense to determine class size based on faculty egos rather than student demand? Does it make sense for professors whose salary comes primarily from tuition dollars to have almost no incentives to deliver a quality education to their students?

I don't think so.

*   *   *

This chapter opened with a look at the longstanding assumption in higher education that student performance in the classroom should naturally follow a bell curve—the idea that roughly 20 percent of students in any educational context will do poorly, at least relative to their classmates. But where did that assumption come from? Why do we assume that talent is arbitrarily scarce and that our role as educators is not so much to educate as it is to create a rank ordering of talent?

Answering that question requires exploring one more source of scarcity—*credentials*. In the factory model of education, we're not just teaching students to edify themselves in some abstract sense. We're "processing" them with the goal of bringing them to market, and that has important implications. If we want our students to beat out the competition and compete successfully in the marketplace for jobs, we have to be able to guarantee to prospective employers that they represent a superior product—that their brand, in other words, is good. That requires credentialing, which is the subject of the next chapter.

5

The Noisy Classroom: What College Diplomas Signal—and the Resulting Distortions

In the movie *Good Will Hunting*, there's a famous scene in which the protagonist, Will Hunting, sees a friend being belittled for his lack of education by an egotistical Harvard student named Clark. Will steps in and belittles Clark in turn for choosing to pursue a college degree. "The sad thing about a guy like you," he says, "is that in fifty years you're going to do some thinking on your own, and you're going to come up with the fact that there are two certainties in life. One: Don't do that. And two: You dropped $150,000 on a fucking education you could have got for $1.50 in late charges at the public library."[1]

Clark is clearly rocked for a moment but then comes back with this: "Yeah, but I *will* have a degree. And you'll be serving my kids fries at a drive-through on our way to a skiing trip."

Welcome to the third stage in the factory model of education—bringing finished products to market.

Many of my colleagues hate that formulation. And I get it. As professors, we don't like thinking of our mission primarily in terms of job-market outcomes. We're conditioned to believe that we—and the universities we're a part of—have a higher purpose, which is to deliver a liberal education that will enable our graduates to be effective members of society, no matter what kind of work they do.

Okay. But let's be honest. A liberal education might be the outcome many educators care about, but it's certainly not the outcome most of our students care about. For better or worse, the vast majority of our students are willing to pay our high tuition prices and take four years out of their lives not because they've always dreamed of becoming learned members of society, but because they know that a college degree is the most reliable path to a well-paying career.

Why is a college degree the most reliable path to a well-paying career? This is where our third scarcity— *credentials*—enters the picture. You see, there are many ways someone might obtain the skills, knowledge, and motivation to succeed in the workplace, but when you begin looking for a job, the best way to signal to employers that you have what they need is to wave around your college degree.

That's the lesson that Clark was snidely trying to teach Will Hunting. College degrees are scarce. College degrees from elite institutions are very scarce. And college degrees from Harvard are *really* scarce. So if you have any one of those, you're sending a signal to potential employers: I have value.

*   *   *

In 2001, three American economics professors—George Akerlof, Joseph Stiglitz, and Michael Spence—were awarded the Nobel Prize in Economics for pioneering work they had done analyzing markets where there is "asymmetric information"—markets where, as the Nobel Committee put it, "actors on one side of the market have much better information than those on the other."[2]

Asymmetries of information exist in many economic transactions. They exist, for example, when the seller of a used car has more information about a car's true quality than the buyer; when the buyer of an insurance policy has more information about their true risk than the company selling the policy; and when a hotelier has more information about the quality of a room than a potential customer. Akerlof, Stiglitz, and Spence studied the problems that can occur in all of these markets, and explained how mechanisms such as used-car warranties, insurance deductibles, and brand advertising can help the more informed party in a transaction communicate their true economic value to the less informed party.

In working on these questions, Michael Spence formalized models of economic signaling and applied them to his own industry—higher education. As the Nobel Committee summarized it, one of his basic ideas was this: even if college coursework has no "intrinsic value" in the job market, a "costly investment in education as such" can signal a student's true ability to potential employers.[3]

In 1973, Spence published a seminal paper on this subject in the *Quarterly Journal of Economics*. In the paper, titled "Job Market Signaling," he considers the asymmetry of information between employers and job applicants, and in one instance creates a simple model of behavior in a job market where there are only two types of applicants—those with high ability (intelligence, motivation) and those with low ability.[4] Information asymmetry exists because only the applicants know their true ability. Employers can ask applicants if they are smart and motivated, but everybody understands that both types of applicants will answer yes.

In working with this model, Spence had an important insight. If obtaining a university degree requires much more time and effort for "low-ability" workers than for "high-ability" workers, then, even though both groups recognize the economic benefit of a degree in terms of higher wages, the highly able workers will be the most likely to choose to complete the degree. Many low-ability workers, on the other hand, will decide that the time and effort required to complete the degree outweigh any salary benefit they might get after graduating. And if mainly high-ability workers choose to earn a degree, then employers can safely assume that if you have a degree, you're probably in the high-ability group.

While this signaling view of degrees doesn't explain everything about the value of college, it explains a lot. First, it helps explain why employers want to know that applicants have passed all sorts of subjects that have

nothing to do with the job for which they're hiring—
Latin, say, or differential equations or organic chemistry. Even if students will never use those skills in their
job, the fact that they had the intelligence and motivation to complete "hard" classes serves as a credible signal that they are likely to make smart and motivated
employees.

Signaling also comes into play when employers place
a much higher value on applicants who have completed
their degree than on those who have dropped out just a
few credits short. Imagine someone who dropped out of
college twelve credits shy of the 120 credits required to
finish her degree, but who up until that point had done
well in all of her classes—and, in fact, had completed
all of the requirements for her major. If she was applying for a job and showed her transcript to a potential
employer, would that employer focus on the 90 percent
of her coursework that she'd completed? Of course not.
The employer would assume that there's something
wrong with her—even if the missing classes have nothing to do with the job she's applying for. Why didn't
she complete her final twelve credits? Is she lazy? Easily
distracted? Does she lack follow through?

Signaling helps explain something else—why employers demand college degrees for all sorts of jobs,
but at the same time complain that colleges are doing
a poor job of preparing students for a career in "the real
world." Apple's Tim Cook, for example, has complained
about the "mismatch between the skills that are coming

out of colleges and what the skills are that we believe we need."[5] IBM's former CEO Ginni Rometty has similarly criticized higher education for "not serving up the people we need."[6]

In the face of widespread skepticism among employers about the skills and preparedness of college graduates, you'd expect that employers would deemphasize college degrees in their hiring practices. In fact, the opposite is true. Studies by Georgetown University's Center on Education and the Workforce found that between 1973 and 2007, the proportion of jobs requiring a college degree increased from 28 percent to 59 percent of all positions,[7] and that by 2020 that number will be 65 percent.[8]

What's even more curious is that many of the jobs requiring a college degree don't seem to require the coursework necessary to get the degree. Burning Glass Technologies collects data about the skills that are in demand in the labor market. When the company recently looked at its data, it found that a bachelor's degree was required for the majority of openings for executive secretaries and executive assistants (65 percent), computer network support specialists (70 percent), and transportation, storage, and distribution managers (74 percent).[9]

Certainly there are a lot of applicants who are perfectly qualified for those roles even though they don't hold a college degree. But if that's true, why do employers require one? According to Burning Glass, it's because they're "relying on a B.A. as a broad recruitment filter that may or may not correspond to specific capabilities needed to do the job." In a story covering the Burning Glass report, the *New York Times* was even more blunt, arguing that "employers assume that people who don't go to college in this day and age must be inferior candidates."[10] In a different article, titled "It Takes a B.A. to Find a Job as a File Clerk," a recruiter told the *Times* that a college degree is little more than a way to filter applicants. "When you get 800 résumés for every job ad," she said, "you need to weed them out somehow."[11]

The signaling view of college degrees might also help explain the curious behavior of university administrators during COVID. In the prior chapter, I chide college leaders who insist that in-person education is much more valuable than online learning but nonetheless didn't lower their university's tuition prices when classes were held remotely during COVID. What's going on there? And why did students and their families put up with it? It sounds like everybody understands that much of the value that students get out of college comes, not from the education they receive on campus, but from the signal their degree confers in the marketplace.

And then there's the class dimension. Federal law prohibits employment discrimination, including selection processes that have a disparate impact on minority groups. These include hiring tests, IQ tests, and physical fitness tests—even those arguably related to job requirements. What's not included—filtering applicants based on whether they have a college degree. As the website *Inside Higher Ed* put it in 2018, "risk-averse employers have become increasingly reliant upon [college degrees] as an expedient way to screen applicants while avoiding the legal pitfalls accompanying other employment tests," even though screening applicants based on degree requirements "disproportionately harms groups with low college graduation rates, particularly blacks and Hispanics."[12]

A 2019 article in the *Chronicle of Higher Education* makes a related point about how signaling by degrees gets in the way of social justice. "Sure," the article states, "having a degree might signal that you're tenacious, communicative, and so on, but given that people who are white and wealthy are more likely to graduate from a four-year institution, it also signals that you come from a certain tier in society."[13]

In other words, you're Clark, not Will Hunting.

*   *   *

The painful reality is that bias is unavoidable when a degree is used as a signal of an individual's true capabilities. That's because, to be effective, the signal doesn't have to be true at the individual level. It just has to be true on average across the population. For a college degree to be a credible signal, not every degree holder has to be smarter, more knowledgeable, or more motivated than every nondegree holder. They just have to possess those traits on average.

The problem is that evaluating people based primarily on their group membership can create a lot of injustice at the individual level. Think about it this way: if it were true, on average, that people wearing overalls and work boots are more likely to rob you than people wearing suits and dress shoes, does that mean it's right as a general rule to favor the latter category of person over the former? Of course not! But isn't that exactly the kind of filtering that employers and society are doing when they require a college degree for positions that don't necessarily need college coursework? And if so, shouldn't that bias make universities at least a bit uncomfortable?

I think so.

More specifically, I think that the presence of asymmetric information in hiring decisions introduces the possibility of three types of bias toward individuals—*credentialism* (a bias toward individuals who have degrees), *elitism* (a bias toward individuals with degrees from elite schools), and *GPA-ism* (a bias toward individuals with high grade-point averages).

At one level, I'm just stating the obvious. Most of us take those three things for granted when thinking about college graduates: we think of them not so much as bias but as evidence of superior skill. But that assumption merits a closer look.

Let's start with credentialism. In a world with abundant information about the true qualities of applicants, employers would be able to recognize when someone who left Carnegie Mellon University just twelve credits short of a degree in computer science was every bit as intelligent, conscientious, and motivated as someone who finished those last twelve credit hours. But in a world of asymmetric information, they understandably assume there is a significant gap in intelligence and motivation between those two applicants.

But is there? For many years, IBM required college degrees for all of its jobs. Recently, to avoid introducing unintentional bias into their hiring practices, IBM deemphasized college credentials to the point where 43 percent of its job openings don't require a four-year degree.[14] According to the company's former CEO and executive chair, Ginni Rometty, the move didn't "dumb down" the pool of employees at all. "Their ability to perform, their curiosity," she said, "matched everyone's."[15] In 2021, IBM's chief human resources officer, Nickle LaMoreaux, summed up the lesson learned. "If you shut the door to talent because it doesn't come with a degree," she said, "you are really closing off your potential for success."[16] And IBM is far from alone in arriving at this conclusion. A 2017 study by Joseph B. Fuller and Manjari Raman of the Harvard Business School surveyed six hundred business and human resources executives and found that "two-thirds of companies acknowledge that stipulating a four-year degree excludes qualified candidates from consideration."[17]

With respect to elitism, scarce information about quality forces employers to make potentially fallacious assumptions about degree holders who happened to graduate from different institutions. A computer science graduate from Alcorn State University or Appalachian State University might be every bit as intelligent, conscientious, and motivated an employee as a computer science graduate from Carnegie Mellon University, but in a world of scarce information about graduates' actual skills, employers favor graduates of elite institutions over those who graduated from less elite institutions.

That's exactly what Lauren Rivera, of Northwestern University's Kellogg School of Management, has found in her work. In researching her book *Pedigree: How Elite Students Get Elite Jobs*, Rivera interviewed 120 decision makers at elite professional service firms who hire candidates for top investment banking, management consulting, and law firm jobs. She found that these hiring managers focus their hiring on the three to five most elite campuses and only occasionally dip their toe into the applications that come from other top-twenty schools. What happens to applicants from other schools? According to one manager, "I'm just being really honest, it pretty much goes into a black hole."[18] Another manager was even more blunt. "We just refuse to look at them."[19]

If all the really good candidates for these jobs were from the top twenty schools, then it might be perfectly reasonable only to consider them. But are graduates of elite schools really in a class above everyone else? A 2021 study published in the *European Journal of*

International Management[20] found only nominal differences in job performance between graduates of elite and other universities.

So why do hiring managers at elite professional service firms not consider potentially qualified applicants from outside the top twenty schools? For the same reason other firms exclude potentially qualified applicants who don't happen to have a college degree: most of the time, these exclusionary policies are right, and they make a hiring manager's job a lot easier. As one investment banker put it to Rivera, "The best kid in the country may be at Bowling Green. But to go to Bowling Green [and] interview twenty kids just to find that one needle in the haystack doesn't make sense, when you can go to Harvard [and have] thirty kids that are all super qualified and great."[21]

Selling elitism might increase the power of elite schools, and buying elitism might make a hiring manager's job easier, but the problem here is that this kind of elitism directly contributes to social injustice. As Rivera wrote in 2015 for the *Harvard Business Review* online:

> Many of the professionals I spoke with lamented a lack of racial diversity in their companies and blamed the applicant "pipeline." But by limiting consideration to students at listed schools, which often have relatively low levels of racial diversity, firms are defining the pipeline in an artificially narrow manner. The career services director of a top MBA program I interviewed put it best when she said, "Firms are scrambling for diversity. They want gender diversity, racial diversity,

you name it, and [they] go to great lengths to attract diverse applicants. They are all fighting for the same tiny piece of the pie. But they are focusing on that slice rather than expanding it, which is the real problem."[22]

The problems are similar when it comes to GPA-ism: scarce information about quality leads employers to assume that a graduate with a 3.5 GPA must be smarter, more knowledgeable, and more motivated than a graduate who has only a 3.0. That's what Google assumed for a long time. The company even required job applicants to provide both their grades and standardized test scores. Then Laszlo Bock, Google's senior vice president for people operations, looked at Google's data and discovered that the signals they were getting from GPAs and standardized test scores filtered out a lot of perfectly qualified applicants. "One of the things we've seen from all our data crunching," he told the *New York Times* in 2013, "is that G.P.A.'s are worthless as a criteria for hiring, and test scores are worthless."[23]

*   *   *

The point here is that, in a world of scarce information about an applicant's true skills, employers are forced to rely on signals of an applicant's intelligence and motivation that don't always reflect the applicant's *actual* intelligence and motivation. It's fair to say that in relying on degrees, reputations, and grades in their hiring decisions, managers select the right candidates most of the time—but in doing so also exclude a lot of talented and motivated individuals who simply lack access to the elite university credentials necessary to signal their true capabilities. Employers do this not because they are callous or cruel, but because sorting students based on limited measures like degrees, reputations, and grades is a better alternative to trying to locate the smart and motivated applicants who might exist somewhere in the uncredentialed pile.

Given the injustices that signals can create, why don't colleges and universities invest in ways to deemphasize the signaling role of credentialism, elitism, and GPA-ism in the job market? The simple answer is that colleges and universities benefit from their role as providers of these signals, and as gatekeepers whose pricey degrees open the door for students to pursue their careers. Their power derives from their ability to provide these valuable signals, even though there are reasonable questions about how accurate those signals actually are in practice, or how many people are unfairly excluded from hiring consideration simply because their social or economic status means they can't send the signal employers are looking for.

In a perfect world, colleges and universities would want to help talented individuals who lack credentials thrive by developing new ways to make information about their true capabilities abundantly available to employers. Unfortunately, we don't live in a perfect world. The world we live in is one in which scarce signaling mechanisms—and the biases associated with them—are key to propagating the business models of many of the 4,500 institutions of higher learning today.

So here we are, well into the twenty-first century and the digital revolution, stuck with a century-old factory model of education that's based on the scarcities we've talked about in the past three chapters—scarcities of access, instruction, and credentials. For a long time, that was the best we could do. But what if now—thanks to new technologies and the possibilities for change that they've opened up—we actually have the chance to design a new model of higher education that's based not on scarcity but abundance? What might that mean?

III
Instruction

6

Open Enrollment: Why—at Last—We Can Do Things Differently

What we've been discussing up until this point has been based on a pretty simple idea—that one way to understand how new technologies might change our system of higher education is to think of higher education as an industry that's subject to market forces, just like any other industry.

If that idea seems sacrilegious to you or makes you feel vaguely uncomfortable, you're not alone. Deep down, a lot of us in academia, especially in the liberal arts, believe that such a perspective is at odds with our mission. We're educators, not businesspeople. We can't distract ourselves with questions of profit and loss, supply and demand, customers and content. We feel that our ultimate goal—as the English professor Mark Edmundson puts it in *Why Teach? In Defense of a Real Education*—is "to expand our minds and deepen our hearts," not "to feed the demands of the American economy."[1]

That's a noble goal. Most of us in higher education would like to believe we're doing our jobs and pursuing our studies in ways that transcend commercial considerations. But are we really in an either/or situation? In a certain sense, thinking of higher education as a business can be dehumanizing. The factory model demands that, in the aggregate, we think of students as raw material to be processed efficiently and then put to use in the economy. It's a model in which, as Edmundson puts it, "We are educated to fill roles . . . tooled to slide into a social machine and function smoothly." That's less than inspiring. And, as we've seen over the last three chapters, it's downright depressing that the factory model, with its focus on inputs and outputs and measurement, has created growing injustices and inequities that are maddeningly at odds with our mission as educators. I'm no fonder of any of this than Edmundson is.

But I think Edmundson and many liberal arts purists are pining for the way things used to be before we made the changes that allowed us to educate our population at scale. They're conceiving of higher education exclusively as a craft-based industry in which production occurs in small batches—as in, say, the batch of a hundred or so minds and hearts the artisans at Harvard expanded and deepened each year in the 1870s.

There's nothing wrong with that kind of education. It's personally enriching and socially valuable. Some students will always want and need it, and we'll always have elite liberal arts colleges and universities more than willing to provide it. But a craft-based model is labor-intensive and expensive, and it won't ever serve the needs of or be accessible to an entire population. That's why we turned to the factory model, which, despite all of its problems and failures, allowed us to expand more minds and deepen more hearts during the past century than we could have in any other way. But when we adopted the factory model, we never intended it to be a replacement for the craft-based model. We adopted it to augment the capabilities and reach of our system of higher education—which it did very successfully. In adopting the factory model, we helped millions of people pursue an education, launch themselves professionally, earn a living, and contribute to a vibrant economy. And in doing so, we exposed a good number of them to a world of ideas and skills that served them not just narrowly, as workers, but also broadly, as human beings.

Because of that, I don't think the solution to our current problems is to turn back the clock, as I suspect a lot of purists would like us to. If we really want to do more with our educational system—if we want to address its growing inequities, if we want education to reach underserved communities from all walks and stages of life, if we want to make the most of what new educational technologies can do for us, if we want to enable new ways for people to communicate their talents to potential employers—then I say it's time once again for us to look to the business world for new ideas. Again, not as replacements for what we've been doing but enhancements that can help us respond to changing market demands and new technological capabilities.

A century or so ago, after undergoing a series of technological, economic, and social transformations, we found that our system of higher education wasn't equipped to meet the rapidly expanding needs of the day, so we looked at how the business world was coping with those transformations—and we adopted the factory model, which allowed us to dramatically increase the number of students we reached. Now, after undergoing a new series of technological, economic, and social transformations, we're finding once again that our model isn't meeting the rapidly expanding needs of the day. The good news is that in the digital age, the business world has generated some revolutionary new ideas and models for making the most of our new moment. Why not see how we might apply them to higher education?

Like Professor Edmundson, I believe that higher education should provide "learning that will help us see the world anew and show us that there could be more to our lives than we had thought." But I don't see why that aspiration should be at odds with higher education adapting to the technological transformations that are occurring in the broader economy, because at least part of what we do is subject to the same economic forces as every other industry—forces that, for the first time in a long time, are changing in fundamental ways.

*   *   *

The scarcity model isn't unique to higher education. For a long time, it has been the defining feature of our economic markets. In just about every industry, those who have succeeded are those who have controlled scarce resources (mining rights, control over market standards, ownership of a brand name) and used them to create value in the marketplace.

The challenge that firms across the economy face today is that digitization is creating abundance in resources that used to be scarce. Think about it: what could be more abundant than digitally encoded information that can be reproduced an infinite number of times, at no additional cost, and without loss of quality? It used to be that an encyclopedia was a $2,000 product with forty thousand entries, but now, thanks to that digital abundance and what it enables, Wikipedia makes six million entries available for free. It used to be that we paid $15 for a single movie on a DVD, but now we can have bundled access to thousands of movies, on demand, for $5 to $10 a month.

That's great for consumers. The problem is that markets based on abundance create enormous challenges for established firms that have structured their entire business around scarcity. If you've always been taught—and have always observed—that scarcity is what creates value (and that your organization needs to protect those scarce resources at all costs), then trying to unlearn that law of scarcity will feel like trying to unlearn, say, the law of gravity.

But unlearn we must. In the digital age, there are plenty of situations in which the old laws of market success no longer apply. Nowhere is this more apparent than in situations where it's now possible to embrace a model of abundance. We in higher education have so far resisted engaging with this idea because it threatens the scarcity-based model we've been using for so long to maintain our power in the market, but, as I argue at the outset of this book, that kind of thinking mistakenly conflates our model with our mission. Part of the reason higher education is contributing to societal injustices is that we're tied to a scarcity-based model—and within that model, inevitably, we've ended up creating a widening gap between winners and losers. For a long time, the factory model was the best we could do if we wanted to reach as many students as we could. But now the new model of abundance from the digital revolution has made it possible for us to close that gap and better achieve our mission—if we're willing to think creatively about how we fulfill that mission.

This might seem like a very theoretical discussion. But it's not. Consider what's been happening in the entertainment industry in recent years. The story is a rich and fascinating one—so much so that a few years ago, my colleague Rahul Telang and I were moved to write a whole book about it titled *Streaming, Sharing, Stealing: Big Data and the Future of Entertainment.*[2]

In highly compressed form, the argument we make in the book goes something like this: Throughout the twentieth century, the entertainment industry was remarkably stable, despite technological innovations that regularly altered the way books, music, movies, and television shows were created, distributed, and consumed. That stability convinced executives that their model was not only the right one but maybe even the only viable one. That kind of thinking bred overconfidence, overpricing, and a predictable overreliance on business models tailored to a physical world. It also bred centralized control by a small number of powerful industry gatekeepers, made it hard for customers to access content on their own schedules, and limited the scope of the audience talented artists could reach, particularly those artists who didn't fit into the established mold of delivery.

Trouble arrived early in the twenty-first century when upstart companies powered by new digital technologies began to challenge the status quo. Entertainment executives reflexively dismissed the threat. Netflix, one of them declared, "is a channel, not an alternative."[3] Amazon Studios, another said, was "in way over their heads."[4] YouTube? No self-respecting artist would ever use a DIY platform to start a career. In 1997, there was also a music executive who heard songs compressed into the MP3 format and exclaimed, "No one is going to listen to that shit!"[5] And recall that in 2013, the chief operating officer of Fox told investors, "People will give up food and a roof over their head before they give up TV."[6]

We all know how that worked out. Between 1999 and 2009, the music industry lost 50 percent of its sales. Between 2014 and 2019, roughly sixteen million American households canceled their cable subscriptions.

The important question is *why*. Why did experienced managers in the entertainment industry miss the threat digital technologies posed to their business? In retrospect, the answer is painfully obvious: they failed to understand that scarce resources were critical to their market power, and that new digital technologies were about to make those scarce resources abundantly available.

In the entertainment industry, major studios, publishers, and music labels maintained their power by controlling three key scarce resources—the financial and technical resources necessary for artists to create content, the channels necessary for artists to reach their audience, and the ways consumers could access that content. This control supported the power of major music labels and motion picture studios in all sorts of ways. The label or studio became *the* source of the money, the equipment, and the studio access necessary for musicians and actors to pursue their creative visions. It became *the* conduit for artists to access the scarce shelf space of record stores and the scarce screens of major theaters. The label or the studio, and only the label or studio, controlled how customers accessed and paid for its content.

Then a new generation of digital technologies made those scarce resources plentiful. In a world of 4K smartphone cameras and inexpensive editing software, artists were no longer dependent on studios or labels to do their craft. Similarly, in a world of self-promotion through social media and self-distribution through digital channels like iTunes, Spotify, and YouTube, artists were no longer dependent on labels and studios for access to their customers. And in a world of abundant access to content, initially through piracy platforms such as Napster, The Pirate Bay, and Megaupload, the majors had to scurry for new ways of making money from customers. These changes forced consumers and artists to start asking discomfiting questions: Why pay CD prices for iTunes downloads that can be reproduced at zero cost? Why keep cable when so many movies and TV shows are available in less expensive and more convenient digital formats? Why sign your life away to a label at all? Why not pitch your new show to Amazon, Apple, or Netflix instead of Paramount, Universal or Warner Brothers?

What's important to understand about this story is that new technologies changed the model for the delivery of entertainment but didn't impede the industry's underlying mission. Books, music, and movies are all still very much with us. The creation of new digital streaming and download platforms didn't spell the end of the entertainment industry. Instead, after an uncomfortable transition period, they produced an explosion in creative output delivered through the convenience, personalization, and interactivity of Kindle libraries, Netflix recommendations, and Spotify playlists. Despite—or maybe because of—the digital disruption we've recently lived through, we're now enjoying a golden age of entertainment where storytelling is available in forms that are serving our needs better than ever before.

What if we could achieve something similar for higher education?

*   *   *

That's not an unreasonable hope. The dynamics at play in higher education today are not unlike those we've seen in entertainment. Universities have long been remarkably stable institutions, and that stability, built on a model of scarcity, has bred overconfidence, over-pricing, and a predictable overreliance on business models tailored to a physical world. But in a world of broadly available online learning—which is the world that the pandemic has sent us hurtling into—those resources are no longer scarce.

Think about it this way. In the traditional campus-based model, an economics professor can give a lecture to at most a few hundred students because that's all a big classroom can hold. But online, that same professor can deliver that same lecture to an unlimited number of students without having to do any extra work and at no extra cost. In that context, could you blame students if they began questioning the need to pay a premium for physical classroom space?

The same holds true when it comes to faculties. Imagine a world in which ten of the country's top history pro-fessors made their lectures and exams available online for a fee that didn't require exclusive matriculation at a single university. Would the relatively inexpensive education you might get in that situation be "worse" than the expensive one you'd get from just one of those professors teaching at their home university?

The seeds for these sorts of developments—and much more—have already been sown widely, and they're starting to grow in a dizzying variety of ways. Udacity, Credly, and Coursera are developing new ways students can certify their skills to employers without having to spend time and money on a traditional college diploma. Outlier, Udemy, and StraighterLine are developing lower-priced options for students to earn transferrable college credits.[7] Arizona State University and Southern New Hampshire University are developing online programs that scale to deliver education to hundreds of thousands of students worldwide. ASU's BioSpine, McGraw Hill's ALEKS, and the Minerva Project are developing ways to use data from online courses to design learning programs that are customized to each individual student's needs, backgrounds, and learning styles—at a scale no individual professor can match.

Novelty is everywhere in this new field of growth. Cengage Unlimited, CodeAcademy, and LinkedIn Learning are creating new, radically lower-priced subscription models for students to pay for their educations. General Assembly, Kenzie Academy, and Lambda School are rethinking our revenue model entirely by allowing students to pay tuition only after they find a job with a good salary in their chosen field.

IBM's Apprenticeship Program,[8] Google's Career Certificates,[9] and Amazon's Technical Academy[10] create opportunities for individuals who may not have traditional university credentials to develop "new-collar" skills in one-to-one relationships with experienced mentors.

Programs like the ones I've just cited are far from perfect. They don't pretend to offer the full suite of courses, experiences, and services that residential colleges and universities do. They don't put students in classrooms with their professors. They don't offer a traditional university diploma or the lifelong friendships and alumni connections that residential programs can provide. If those are the things you're looking for, you're inevitably going to conclude—as many of my colleagues in academia have—that these new programs are inferior and pose no serious threat to higher education as we know it. To pick an example almost at random, here's how Donald Eastman, the president of Eckerd College, dismissed these sorts of programs in 2013. "It is nonsense," he said, "for any public or private university to pretend that online courses for undergraduate students provide quality education."[11] (During the pandemic, when Eckerd switched to online courses, Eastman nevertheless denied students tuition refunds because, as his communications staff put it, "Eckerd's education will continue to be high quality and high impact, even at a distance.")[12]

These new programs may not be able to do it all, but they are unbundling key pieces of our core educational mission, and they're doing it using models of abundance that allow them to reach many more students, of all ages and economic backgrounds, at a far lower cost. What they lack in quality they make up in convenience—and as they get more popular, they're only going to become better. How many people today still listen to CDs?

It's worth noting, though, that books, music, movies, and TV shows are all still very much with us. Despite— or, in my view, because of—all the digital disruption we've recently lived through, we've seen an explosion in choices for both artists and consumers. Top 40 radio and prime-time television are still with us, but artists whose creative vision doesn't fit in the narrow constraints of those formats are now able to pursue their craft on new platforms such as Netflix, Spotify, TikTok, and YouTube and even on innovative new platforms fostered by industry stalwarts such as Disney+, HBOMax, and Hulu.

I envisage a similar future for higher education. In so many ways, we're now living in an age of abundance, not scarcity, and it's time to reimagine our model of higher education accordingly. What if, no longer constrained by the three scarcities that have for so long formed the basis of our current system, we could design a system that's more accessible, equitable, and just?

*   *   *

The rest of this book explores what such a system might look like. It looks at how new technologies have recently given us the ability to radically change and expand our model of higher education, and it shows that by embracing the potential of new technologies, we can introduce new ways for educators to convey their expertise, for students to achieve mastery over materials, and for employers to discover and develop previously untapped talent.

This is not an either-or situation. The new technologies and models that I discuss in the pages ahead will not make traditional colleges and universities disappear. If you have the money, the pedigree, and the desire to go to, say, Colby or Tulane or UC-Berkeley, you'll still be able to do that. Exclusive institutions of higher learning will continue to do what they've always done—serve an elite portion of the population very well. But if I'm right, fewer and fewer students will need to attend those institutions because new technologies and ideas will make a new set of creative, personalized, and dramatically less expensive ways of learning available to them—and to all sorts of other people who are now excluded from our system of higher education.

Isn't that something we should all want?

The Digitally Powered Ivory Tower: How Digitization Is Creating Abundance in Access and Instruction

As the new millennium began, institutions of higher learning started to embrace these new opportunities for abundance. The process began in earnest when some took their residential degree programs online.

That's what Paul LeBlanc did at Southern New Hampshire University, a small private university in Manchester, New Hampshire. When LeBlanc was named SNHU's president in 2003, the school's future looked grim. Its enrollment and endowment were dwindling, and it was teetering on the verge of financial collapse. But in the past two decades, LeBlanc has engineered an almost miraculous turnaround. Today, SNHU is the largest accredited university in the United States, and the fastest-growing. Since 2003, its enrollment has increased from 3,000 to 175,000. Yes, you read that right—175,000 students.

How did LeBlanc accomplish this astonishing feat? With a simple plan: move course offerings online, and focus on the needs of nontraditional learners.

At the time LeBlanc took over, almost all universities were designed to serve the needs of students who were coming straight out of high school and who could enroll full time at a residential university.[1] But those students comprised only 20 percent of all students. What about the remaining 80 percent—the "nontraditional learners," many of them adults who couldn't afford to pay for a residential program or leave their jobs and families to enroll in one?

This population, LeBlanc recognized, represented a significantly underserved market. "The world in which we live equally distributes talent," he later told a graduating class at SNHU, "but it doesn't equally distribute opportunity, and paths are not always the same."[2]

With that idea as his guiding principle, LeBlanc set out to reinvent SNHU to serve the needs of nontraditional learners, and in so doing launched the university's remarkable turnaround.[3] His plan hinged on offering classes and degrees online at a cost that was substantially lower than residential classes and degrees, and on making enrollment open to anybody with a high school diploma or GED. The classes would be planned centrally by subject-matter experts and then delivered digitally by a small army of adjunct professors.

That's the model still in place today. The classes, now taught by more than six thousand professors, involve a mix of readings, short video instruction (mostly under five minutes), and practice problems. Students interact with instructors and classmates through online discussion boards and over email.

Since 2012, SNHU has also offered a competency-based program that represents a distinct break with the idea of "seat time" that pervades the factory model of higher education. Known as College for America, and launched in partnership with the Bill and Melinda Gates Foundation, the program allows working adults to receive credit for demonstrated mastery of a subject—even if that mastery came from work experience rather than time in a traditional classroom.[4]

With classes online, LeBlanc realized that by combining the data generated across SNHU's online classes with predictive analytics, he could identify students who were struggling and might need extra support. In a traditional environment, these students would likely slip through the cracks. Sure, individual professors might recognize that a student was struggling in their class, but no one would have the whole picture on the student until the end of the semester when grades were in and it was too late. SNHU used its data to identify at-risk students early and reach out to them directly, even at times calling them at home to ask if they needed extra support.[5] "We are super-focused on customer service," LeBlanc said in 2014, "which is a phrase that most universities can't even use."[6]

LeBlanc knew that to serve nontraditional students he would have to keep tuition prices low. And he did so. In 2011, LeBlanc set SNHU's online tuition at $320 per credit hour, allowing students to complete a 120-credit, four-year bachelor's degree for less than $10,000 per year. That was an incredibly low price in 2011, but what's even more surprising is that between 2011 and 2021, a period when private four-year institutions raised prices by 40 percent,[7] SNHU's tuition stayed exactly the same.[8]

With many traditional universities struggling financially, you might think that not raising tuition for over a decade would have hurt SNHU's finances. You'd be wrong. The school maintains a 24 percent margin on its online classes, and with 97 percent of its students online, the school reported a $60 million surplus on a $1 billion budget in 2020.[9]

If SNHU were a for-profit institution, it would have to decide whether to exploit its high margins for the benefit of its investors or use them for the benefit of its students—a conflict that has plagued many for-profit educational institutions. As a nonprofit, SNHU faced no such quandary and was able to focus on delivering benefits to its students—including residential students. In 2017, SNHU added a freeze on residential tuition to the tuition freeze already on online tuition.[10] And in 2021, the school announced that it was *cutting* residential tuition rates by more than half, from $31,000 to $15,000 for face-to-face instruction and to $10,000 for a mix of face-to-face and online instruction.[11]

As a child who grew up on a subsistence farm in New Brunswick, Canada,[12] LeBlanc understood how important it was to keep tuition prices low for underprivileged students. But how did he manage to do it if, as is noted in chapter 1, Baumol's cost disease inexorably causes the price of higher education to rise?

This is a good question—if you're talking about a situation in which faculty productivity is static while labor productivity rises in other sectors of the economy. That's the case in the traditional model of education: professors in the classroom today still need about the same amount of time to teach the same number of students as they have done for decades, even as workers in other sectors have grown more efficient. But the equation changes when a single professor can reach thousands of students, as is the case in online education. In that situation, faculty productivity rises dramatically, and Baumol's cost disease is no longer an issue.

In moving to an online delivery model, SNHU dramatically broadened its reach, and in doing so, it created two kinds of abundance for its students—abundance in access (open enrollment, lower prices, and improved customer service for nontraditional applicants) and abundance in instruction (online learning, data analysis, and competency-based advancement). In 2012, acknowledging what SNHU had already accomplished, *Fast Company* magazine named it the twelfth most innovative organization in the world. And every year since 2015, *U.S. News* has named it one of the country's most innovative colleges and universities.[13]

Other schools have followed suit, among them Arizona State University, Liberty University, and Western

Governors University. All of these institutions target working adults who don't fit the mold of traditional residential programs, allowing tens of thousands of these students to achieve their college aspirations at a fraction of the price of traditional residential programs. In February 2019, the *Chronicle of Higher Education* reported on the extent of this trend in an article aptly titled "The Rise of the Mega-University."[14]

I can imagine many colleagues rolling their eyes at this point, saying that the online education offered by these lower-tier institutions doesn't measure up to the high-quality, residential education available from elite colleges and universities and that technological innovations will never make up for that.

I disagree. Those who dismiss the quality of the online degrees offered by "mega-universities," or whatever they're called, are focusing exclusively on the way value is delivered in residential education and ignoring the many new sources of value that these technological innovations offer to students—increased flexibility, increased customizability, reduced time, and radically lower cost. Those innovations are going to help a lot of people, and as more people take advantage of them, they're going to get better and better, and their benefits will become more and more obvious. It was easy for record companies initially to dismiss the sound quality of MP3s ("Nobody's going to listen to that shit!"), but we all know how that worked out. I see no reason why something similar won't happen in the world of education.

There's another reason my colleagues shouldn't roll their eyes. After a slow start, elite institutions are getting into the game too.

*   *   *

On August 16, 2011, Stanford University announced that it planned to deliver its three most popular computer science courses online, for free, during the fall semester. The classes were Machine Learning taught by Daphne Koller and Andrew Ng, Introduction to Artificial Intelligence taught by Sebastian Thrun and Peter Norvig, and Introduction to Databases taught by Jennifer Widom.[15]

Stanford expected that a few thousand students would register for the courses. Its estimate was off by a couple of orders of magnitude. In the end, 160,000 students from 209 countries registered for Thrun and Norvig's AI course, and more than 100,000 students registered for Koller and Ng's and Widom's courses, two-thirds of whom came from outside the United States. Many of those students didn't complete the courses, but at the end of the ten-week class sessions, 23,000 students had passed Thrun and Norvig's course, 13,000 had passed Koller and Ng's, and 7,000 had passed Widom's, with each student receiving a statement of accomplishment from Stanford.[16]

It's hard to understate the importance of what had happened. Despite the high dropout rate, five professors in just ten weeks had made it possible for 43,000 students around the world to master the content in Stanford's three most popular computer science classes. In a traditional hundred-person lecture-style classroom, it would take more than 430 professors to educate the same number of students—and that's assuming a 100 percent pass rate. Five professors doing the work of 430 is a phenomenal increase in productivity in an industry where productivity has been more or less stagnant for hundreds of years.

At about the same time but on the other side of the country, a professor at another elite university was conducting a similar experiment. Anant Agarwal of the Massachusetts Institute of Technology decided to deliver one of his undergraduate classes online, also for free. The class, Circuits and Electronics, was known as one of the hardest at MIT, and Agarwal intended to hold students who took it online to the same "MIT-hard" standards as he did to students who took it in person.[17] He expected that a total of about two thousand students would register—but he, too, saw an overwhelmingly enthusiastic surge of interest as soon as he opened registration.[18] In the first hour alone, some 10,000 students signed up for the class, and in the end, nearly 155,000 students from 162 countries did so. Of that number, 7,157 passed the course, earning a certificate of accomplishment from MIT. Recollecting the experience during a 2014 TED Talk, Agarwal observed, "If I were to teach at MIT two semesters every year, I would have to teach for forty years before I could teach this many students."[19]

Seeing the potential for online education to reach more students than they could ever reach through residential instruction, these professors moved from experimentation to implementation. In January 2012, Koller and Ng founded Coursera, which has teamed up with two hundred partner institutions—among them not just Stanford but also Duke, NYU, Yale, and, yes, Carnegie Mellon—to offer three thousand courses that now educate more than ninety-two million students.[20] In February 2012, Sebastian Thrun and his colleagues founded Udacity.com, which has delivered lifelong learning opportunities to over fourteen million students worldwide.[21] And in May 2012, Anant Agarwal became the first president of edX, which has teamed up with 160 partner institutions—among them not only MIT but also Cornell, Dartmouth, Harvard, Princeton, and the University of California at Berkeley—to offer more than 3,600 courses that have been accessed by more than forty-two million students.[22] Later that year, the *New York Times* declared 2012 "The Year of the MOOC," an acronym for massive open online courses—courses that are offered for free and available to anyone with a desire to learn.[23]

These early MOOC pioneers saw free and open access to higher education as a moral issue. At the 2015 Open edX conference, Agarwal observed that education was a "basic right for all humans" and therefore that "anybody in the world should be able to take a course for free."[24] Koller's motivation was similar. In response to a question at the University of Virginia's Darden School of Business about whether Coursera should charge a small fee, say $5, to access its courses instead of making its content available for free, she framed free education as a "moral question." "Five dollars might not be a lot for somebody here sitting in this room," she said, "but it's a heck of a lot of money for a kid in Africa."[25]

*   *   *

If you've paid attention to the debate about MOOCs, you'll know that opponents to them make a lot of noise about their completion rates, which are paltry by the standards of traditional universities. Completion rates in the 4 percent to 5 percent range are common. That represents a pitiful failure, doesn't it? Surely no respectable university could stay in business if 95 percent of its students failed to complete their classes.

Sure, that's true for the traditional model of higher education. But the problem with this objection is that it's applying scarcity-based metrics of physical classrooms to a new model, MOOCs, in which access and instruction are abundant.

Think about it this way. When access to the classroom is scarce, as it is in the traditional model, it makes perfect sense to measure success based on completion rates. But do those metrics make sense when applied to an open, digital classroom? No! Students who drop out of an online class don't keep another student from registering, so they impose no cost on other students who want to access the material. Likewise, when education is offered for free, a student who doesn't complete the class incurs no cost other than the time invested in the class.

We have to devise different measures of success for abundance-based education. They should be based on—well, abundance. One such measure is the number of students who now have an opportunity to master advanced college material who otherwise wouldn't have been given that opportunity.

Consider Battushig Myanganbayar. When Anant Agarwal released his Circuits and Electronics course online, Battushig was a fifteen-year-old high school student in Mongolia. After a teacher at his high school in Ulan Bator introduced him to the class, Battushig signed up—and went on to become one of the 340 students worldwide that semester who earned a perfect score in the class.[26] Think about that. In one semester alone, 340 students around the world, most of them students who would never be able to go to MIT, received perfect scores in one of the university's hardest classes.

Or consider Khushbakht Awan,[27] a housewife in Peshawar, Pakistan. Married in the ninth grade, she decided to go back to school in her twenties, and started by taking Justice, a famous course taught on edX by the renowned Harvard professor Michael Sandel. In a blog post, Awan described the experience, which she never could have had in person, as "a dream come true."[28]

These are the kinds of students that Stanford's Daphne Koller was hoping to reach when she began teaching online. Instead of delivering a Stanford-quality education to a small number of "highly privileged" residential students, as she put it, she wanted "students from every country, every age group, and every walk of life" to have access to Stanford-quality instruction.[29] By that measure, she and others who are now offering free courses online are doing very well.

*   *   *

One might think that creating abundance in access would create problems with instruction. By admitting students who don't have the right grades or test scores, you might end up with people who aren't sufficiently prepared—or smart. At the very least, you are going to find a wide range of skill levels in the classroom, and we've already talked about how hard it is to deliver a quality educational experience to students who have radically different backgrounds and skill levels. Won't instruction suffer when access is abundant?

This objection brings us to how pedagogy changes when instruction becomes abundant.

Online educators discovered that digital delivery gave them opportunities to change how education was delivered. In fact, they discovered that it was *necessary* to change traditional pedagogy when moving from a traditional classroom to online.

One such change was that instead of teaching classes in fixed sixty- to eighty-minute sessions, they began breaking up their instruction into much shorter segments, typically of no more than ten minutes, which they followed with in-video quizzes to ensure that students understood the material before moving on to the next segment.[30] To a degree, this kind of regular assessment is also possible during in-person lecture-based classes, but it's not possible to check in with every student at every step along the way. Shy students and students who might take a little longer to form their thoughts are therefore consistently left behind, as are learners who might take a little longer to master a particular topic.

But can online videos provide the same sort of student connection that in-person education can? Peter Norvig and Sebastian Thrun were surprised to find that they could. One student emailed Norvig that his online videos "felt like sitting in a bar with a really smart friend who's explaining something you haven't grasped, but are about to."[31] Another student emailed Thrun that his online classes felt "more intimate than most of the lectures I attended in the past" and made him "feel that you both were personally tutoring me."[32]

Although online delivery might work for some classes, it will never be possible for classes with a significant in-person laboratory component, right? For example, a class like organic chemistry is exactly the sort of class that won't work online given the need for students to work in sophisticated laboratory environments, not to mention the infeasibility of mailing dangerous hydrochloric acid to a student's home or expecting students to have access to fume hoods or eyewash stations.

That's what Arizona State University professor Ara Austin initially thought about teaching organic chemistry online. What she realized, however, is much of the classroom-based material still could be delivered online. The solution for the laboratory component? Instead of spreading the eight to ten in-person lab exercises throughout the semester, when Austin and her ASU colleagues teach organic chemistry online, they bring students to the Tempe campus for a one-week intensive lab experience. During that week, students spend nearly all their time in the lab with other students in their cohort—three to four hours in the morning, followed by a break, followed by another three to four hours in the afternoon, for seven days nonstop.

How well does this work? Austin and her colleagues Ian Gould and Smitha Pillai studied that question across multiple years from 2018 to 2021 by measuring student outcomes via survey instruments. In a paper titled "Student Outcomes in a Concentrated Chemistry Laboratory Course for Online Students," they measured student outcomes along three dimensions—knowledge, motivation, and identity as scientists. They found that online organic chemistry students performed as well as their in-person counterparts in terms of their knowledge of laboratory skills. And their scientific motivation and identity was, if anything, better.

Why was this so? Having an intensive lab experience, it seems, produced a much stronger scientific motivation and identity among students than having labs that were spread throughout the semester and interspersed with other classes. Their conclusion:

> The intensive organic chemistry laboratory courses are truly an immersive experience that provide not only hands-on skills to online students but also a chance for them to meaningfully connect with their peers and faculty. The majority of our online students are adult learners who cannot attend semester-long laboratory courses due to professional and personal obligations, and this novel approach provides them with a rich experience that leads to equivalent outcomes as their on-campus counterparts.

*   *   *

Online teaching also made other kinds of abundance possible in instruction. One was the ability to scale up to meet demand. When Anant Agarwal realized that not 2,000 but 155,000 students had signed up for his circuits class, he didn't put 153,000 of them on a waiting list. Instead, he asked his technical staff to allocate space for two hundred additional virtual servers, already available on MIT's cloud infrastructure, to deliver the content. A few keystrokes later, the classroom capacity had increased nearly a hundred-fold, at almost no additional cost.[33] Try doing that in a traditional classroom.

Another kind of abundance was the use of technology to reach students who don't speak English. Sebastian Thrun and Peter Norvig used a volunteer army of two thousand translators to make their Introduction to Artificial Intelligence class available in forty-four different languages, creating abundance in instruction for the millions of people worldwide who don't speak English.[34]

A third was the ability to provide personalized feedback. You might think that this would be impossible at the scale of 150,000 students. That was certainly Agarwal's fear before he started teaching his first class. He and his teaching assistants had experience answering questions from a hundred students, but how could they do it for 150,000? Agarwal anticipated that he and his team would be monitoring the forum and answering questions around the clock. But that's not what happened.

One night soon after the course launched, Agarwal realized that things were going to go very differently. He was up at 2 a.m. monitoring the forum, and a question came in from a student in Pakistan. As Agarwal has recalled, it was a watershed moment: "I said, 'Okay, let me go and type up an answer.' I don't type all that fast, and I begin typing up the answer, and before I can finish, another student from Egypt popped in with an answer, not quite right. So I'm fixing the answer, and before I can finish, a student from the U.S. had popped in with a different answer. And then I sat back, fascinated. Boom, boom, boom, boom—the students were discussing and interacting with each other . . . and by 4 a.m. in the morning, they had discovered the right answer. And all I had to do was go and bless it: 'Good answer.'"[35]

Let's pause for a second to reflect on what this means for delivering quality education at scale. In a physical world, the quality of feedback generally decreases with scale: smaller classes are better than larger classes because each student has more access to the scarce faculty expert. Agarwal's observation suggests that the quality of feedback might *increase* with scale when education is delivered online.

Of course, individual feedback might work in an online discussion forum, but is it really possible for graded assignments? No problem, according to Mike Schatz, a professor at Georgia Tech who teaches a course on Coursera titled Introductory Physics with Laboratory. To teach the class, Schatz had to solve the problem of conducting a physics laboratory remotely with students from around the world who don't have access to a proper lab or even a common set of materials. Schatz's solution was to have students use a cell phone camera to record and submit their lab experiments for projectiles in motion and then to use special image processing software, which he himself developed, to automatically evaluate the measurements that students recorded in their lab assignments.[36] Similarly, professors from Rice

University have developed a Python interpreter that provides students in their Coursera Python class with immediate feedback on their coding assignments.[37]

This kind of immediacy matters. According to Daphne Koller and her team at Coursera, when students receive immediate feedback on concepts they might have missed in an assignment, they are much more likely to advance in their learning by trying to answer similar questions until they get it right. Koller calls this phenomenon "self-induced mastery learning."[38]

What we've been discussing so far are assignments in which objective "correct" answers exist. But feedback at scale on work that has to be evaluated subjectively is also possible in the new world of online education. This is where something Koller and Ng call "calibrated peer grading" comes into play.[39] The technique involves giving students a specific grading rubric and asking them to grade their classmates' assignments. And it seems to work well. When Matthew Sakganik and Mitch Duneier of Princeton University studied the calibrated peer grading of the three essay questions they had assigned in their Coursera Sociology course, they found them to be indistinguishable from grades assigned by trained teaching assistants.[40] According to Koller, peer grading has another enormous benefit: students "learn as much from grading the work of others," she has noted, "as they do from doing the work themselves."[41]

So it's possible to evaluate student assignments at scale, but what about delivering high-quality instruction at scale? In the fall of 2012, Khosrow Ghadiri, a professor of electrical engineering at San Jose State University, decided to carry out a daring test. Was it possible, Ghadiri wondered, that his students might actually learn more from Anant Agarwal's online lectures on circuits than from his own in-person lectures on the subject?

To test this hypothesis, Ghadiri chose eighty-six students at random from his class of 236 students and had them sit through Agarwal's lectures instead of his own. The remaining 150 students he taught in person himself. Ghadiri's class is one of the hardest classes in San Jose State's electrical engineering program. In the years prior to Ghadiri's experiment, roughly 40 percent of the students in the class failed. For the eighty-six students who were shown Agarwal's lectures, however, the failure rate was only 9 percent.[42] Two years later, when Ghadiri conducted the experiment again, the failure rate for students taught using Agarwal's lecture had dropped to just 2 percent.[43]

Teaching at scale has still other benefits. It can help professors recognize when students are having conceptual problems. In one of Koller and Ng's machine learning assignments, 2,000 out of the 100,000 students in the class submitted exactly the same wrong answer. That's a ratio of two out of a hundred, which is unlikely to attract any notice in a class of a hundred students. But, according to Ng, "when 2,000 out of 100,000 students submitted the wrong answer to a problem, it was a very clear signal to me that I had done something wrong." Ng and Koller therefore devised an automated system in which, when lots of students all came up with same wrong answer, they would get a custom message that told them to review two steps in particular. That message, Ng has said, allowed students "to much more quickly get over the conceptual error."[44]

And then there's something that Agarwal calls "inverted admissions," in which universities offer admission to their residential programs based on students' performance in online courses rather than on weaker measures of talent such as high school grades and standardized test scores. Indeed, that's how MIT discovered Battushig Myanganbayar from Mongolia. After noticing Myanganbayar's flawless performance online in Circuits and Electronics, the university offered him admission to its residential program. By 2018, he had completed a BS in electrical engineering and computer science *and* an MS in engineering and artificial intelligence—both with a GPA of 5.0.[45]

*   *   *

Way back in 2001, Woodie Flowers, a professor of mechanical engineering, made a prescient statement. "The best lecture I have ever given," he said, "would be no competition for a professionally produced new-media version covering the same material, especially if that material were always instantaneously available to the learner in the style she or he preferred."[46]

For years, nothing much happened on that front. But recently, the entrepreneur Aaron Rasmussen has taken that idea and run with it by launching the online educational platform Outlier. When he launched Outlier, in 2019, Rasmussen already had plenty of experience producing high-quality educational videos. He was cofounder and former creative director at Master-Class, which for a fee offers access to expertly produced video courses in such fields as acting, writing, music, photography, sports, science, design, and business, all taught by the world's leading practitioners. As you may recall, I open this book with a brief discussion of the writing course that Joyce Carol Oates produced with MasterClass.

Rasmussen wanted to bring a MasterClass-style of production to for-credit instruction online. The idea was to offer students engaging, top-quality introductory courses that they could take at low cost and then use to transfer into traditional four-year undergraduate programs—without having to pay for four years of tuition. Like Paul LeBlanc, Rasmussen was motivated to keep tuition costs low based on his own experience.[47] He had attended Boston University on a Pell Grant and made ends meet by taking classes over the summers at a community college close to his home and transferring those credits to Boston University.[48] "I saved thousands of dollars and the credits counted exactly the same as those from Boston University," he later observed.[49]

Rasmussen imagined that Outlier could become something like an online community college that accomplishes many goals at once: it would offer students access to better professors and better instruction than most community colleges could; it would allow them to earn course credits that they could transfer to traditional four-year institutions; and, ultimately, because of those transfer credits, it would allow them to earn an undergraduate degree from one of those institutions at a much lower cost.

Rasmussen found an ally for this vision in Ann Cudd, the provost and vice chancellor of the University of Pittsburgh, who saw a partnership with Outlier as "a gateway for transfer students to Pitt" and as a way for Pitt to enhance college "access and affordability."[50] The ability to earn course credits at Pitt would also allow students to transfer those credits to any degree-granting university that accepted transfer credits from Pitt.

The first class that Rasmussen created for Outlier was Calculus I. He began there in part because of an observation that Woodie Flowers had made in 2012 about the amount of money wasted each year on calculus classes.[51] Writing in an MIT newsletter, Flowers noted that about 40 percent of the 600,000 students who took Calculus I each year were failing the class. If you assume an average cost of about $2,000 per class, he wrote, that translates to about $500 million wasted on in-person Calculus I instruction each year. Rasmussen found that appalling. When he updated the numbers, assuming one million students per year at a cost of $2,500 per class, he came up with an estimate of $1 billion wasted per year on in-person instruction for Calculus I alone.[52] Wouldn't it be better, he thought, to spend $10 million and create an online version of the course that could educate students far more effectively at a small fraction of the cost?

When Outlier launched, it offered both Calculus I and Introduction to Psychology, each priced at $400, less than a sixth of the cost of those courses for students enrolled in the University of Pittsburgh's residential program.[53] The classes also came with something that no university offers—a full refund for students who "do the work but don't pass."[54]

Like the courses on edX and Coursera, Outlier's classes create abundance in access by removing formal application processes and demands for high standardized test scores. For example, enrolling in Outlier's calculus class doesn't require students to demonstrate that they have passed precalculus from an accredited institution or to present their math scores on the SAT. All it requires is that they complete a ten-question pretest with a score of 70 percent or better.

Outlier courses offer several other features not available in residential courses. The first is diversity in faculty expertise. Outlier's calculus class is taught by three different professors—Tim Chartier of Davidson College; Hannah Fry of University College London; and John Urschel, an African American scholar and 2021 graduate of MIT's PhD program in mathematics, who happens to be a former starting guard for the NFL's Baltimore Ravens. These instructors cover the same topics using examples drawn from their own research and experience. For example, Hannah Fry motivates exponential functions from the perspective of her research into happiness, using the example of how the marginal enjoyment of a task, such as cleaning your room, declines over time. Presenting the same topic, John Urschel uses the example of the exponential decay rate in the number of fans for the Buffalo Bills, the team he rooted for as a child, and Tim Chartier uses the exponential increase in the number of retweets for a viral post on Twitter.

The second feature not available in residential courses is diversity in race and gender. Outlier's initial classes in calculus and psychology both had at least one woman and one African American as professors. By 2021, Outlier had expanded to a total of nine classes, adding classes in precalculus, college algebra, astronomy, statistics, philosophy, microeconomics, and macroeconomics. Each course had at least one woman professor, and six of the nine had at least one African American. All told, half of Outlier's instructors in 2021 were women, 42 percent of whom belong to a racial minority; 20 percent were African American; and 8 percent were Hispanic. Each of these proportions exceed, in some cases by a wide margin, the diversity of professors on US college campuses.[55]

How might this create abundance in instruction? Recall that we talked about the improved performance seen when women in STEM fields can receive instruction from other women and when underrepresented minorities can receive instruction from instructors who look like them. Online education can deliver that. Hannah Fry, for example, is very likely to inspire many female students in the STEM fields who would never have the opportunity to take her classes at University College in London. And John Urschel is very likely to do the same for students of color in STEM fields who don't have the opportunity to take his classes at MIT.

I hope you'll recognize that I'm not arguing here that online education is better than residential for all students or in all contexts. The point I'm trying to make is simply that online education might benefit *some* students in *some* contexts, and that we in higher education shouldn't stand in the way of providing access to those students by arguing that residential education is better than online education for all students in all contexts—an argument that I'm afraid I've heard regularly when online education comes up in my discussions with faculty.

*   *   *

The watershed moment for online education came during the COVID-19 lockdown. Suddenly, without any time to prepare, college professors had to switch to remote learning, and we were all forced to question long-held assumptions about what's possible in the online classroom.

I certainly was. I love in-person teaching. There's something almost magical about the energy you can generate in the classroom—energy that's hard to replicate online. Face-to-face interaction between teachers and students *matters*. Without the social and motivational cues of the classroom, students can have a hard time focusing, especially when nobody can tell if they're paying attention to the class or watching a YouTube video.

At the same time, I've heard from both students and instructors about many aspects of the online experience during the lockdown that they found beneficial. Many students appreciated the ability to review recorded lectures for topics they might have missed the first time. Other students—particularly those who were shy about raising their hands in class—appreciated the ability to ask and answer questions in the Zoom chat. Reviewing chat transcripts briefly during class, and in more detail after class, I was regularly shocked—and delighted—by the amount of student-led interaction and learning that occurred when students were able to ask and answer one another's questions on the fly. That kind of learning in parallel is hard to replicate during in-person lectures.

I also appreciated the ability to create on-the-fly breakout rooms to seed discussions on particularly complicated subjects. These breakout discussions allowed some students to gain enough confidence from sharing their ideas in a small group to later share those ideas with the entire class—to everyone's benefit.

Guest lecturers were another wonderful and surprising benefit of online instruction. It turns out that it's far easier to persuade a busy executive or expert to visit class when, instead of asking them to take two days out of their schedule to fly to Pittsburgh, you ask for eighty minutes of their time to join a Zoom call. When I taught remotely, I brought in famous authors, senior executives, and prominent entrepreneurs to talk about how their real-world experiences related to topics the students were discussing in class. I was even able to bring in two experts to debate different sides of a complicated policy question, allowing students to make decisions for themselves based on the best arguments out there, as opposed to making decisions through the lens of my (somewhat biased) thoughts on the topic. Teaching this way made me feel less like a one-man band and more like a conductor.

Other colleagues I've spoken to have told me that when they taught online, they were able to use new data sources to customize the education they delivered to meet the needs of individual students and to create a better overall learning environment than they could in the one-size-fits-all model of classroom instruction.

For example, Jim Jordan, a Carnegie Mellon colleague of mine who teaches Introduction to Finance and Accounting, told me that he has been amazed at how much better a teacher he can be online versus in the classroom. In an online classroom, he's able to use software to keep track of how each student in the class is interacting with the online material. The software allows him to introduce adaptive quizzes into the online lectures—quizzes that identify conceptual problems that students might be having, and then suggest particular topics or lessons to review. The software also gives him a dashboard view of the class where he can see, at the class and individual levels, how much time students are spending on the platform—reviewing class materials and lectures, doing homework, and taking quizzes.

With this extra information, Jordan was able to quickly identify and adapt assignments that weren't teaching students well. He was also able to quickly identify students who were having trouble with the material or getting stuck, and to reach out to them in a way that he couldn't when the class was taught in person. He was even able to make an important distinction between students and their individual needs: those who spent little time reviewing class materials but did well on the assessments probably knew the material already, which meant he could reach out to them with more advanced materials, whereas those who spent a lot of time reviewing the class materials and did poorly on assessments probably needed a different sort of intervention to help them improve.

A different professor, from a top business school, recently mentioned to me that she had been surprised to discover another benefit of online instruction—increased classroom diversity. Her school is very proud and protective of the quality of its in-person instruction—including a long-standing eight-week residential executive education program. The school long believed that that program had to be taught in person because of the importance of face-to-face interactions to creating community. The program had been a success when taught in-person, but it had long had one big problem: women just didn't seem to want to apply, even when the school targeted them for enrollment. During COVID, the school took that class online, and there was a huge increase in the number of female executives who registered. This was an "aha" moment for the school. By requiring residential attendance, it turned out, they were excluding a lot of women executives who were less able than their male counterparts to leave their families for eight weeks. Since figuring this out, the school has decided to keep the program online.

As the *New York Times* reported in August 2021, online learning has helped many students with disabilities pursue their educations too.[56] One of the students profiled in the article, Daniel Goldberg, has chronic inflammatory bowel disease and before COVID frequently had to miss in-person classes because of this condition. During COVID, he didn't miss a single class. Other students profiled in the article had different disabilities, each of which had always made in-person learning difficult, and they, like Goldberg, had benefitted greatly from being able to study remotely. Why, they all wondered, should any disability—whether it's spinal muscular atrophy, muscular dystrophy, sickle-cell disease, celiac disease, diabetes, or anything else—stand in the way of anybody's educational dreams?

*   *   *

The idea of using technology to create a lower-priced and more-accessible system of higher education sounds great. But you may be thinking that it also sounds very familiar. The basic capabilities described in this chapter, after all, have been around for at least the past ten years. Sure, they've evolved and improved over time, but they haven't resulted in the fundamental changes that many predicted.

There were certainly a lot of heady predictions. In May 2012, in a *New York Times* article titled "The Campus Tsunami," David Brooks declared, "What happened to the newspaper and magazine business is about to happen to higher education: a rescrambling around the Web."[57] In July of that same year, William Bennett, a former secretary of education, predicted that MOOCs were "in the process of revolutionizing higher education in a way that educators, colleges and universities cannot, or will not."[58] And in November, in another *Times* article, titled "The Year of the MOOC," Anant Agarwal was quoted as saying, "I like to call this the year of disruption and the year is not over yet."[59] Less than two years later, in May 2014, Clay Christensen of Harvard Business

School made perhaps the most provocative statement of all. In a keynote address that he delivered at a Colgate University conference titled "Innovation and Disruption in Higher Education," Christensen declared that it was his sense that "within ten to fifteen years, maybe as many as half of our universities will be in the business of being liquidated or getting out of bankruptcy."[60]

But here we are, a decade or so later, and the promised disruption has yet to arrive. When it comes to the powerful position colleges and universities hold in the market for higher education, things are pretty much the same as they've always been. Which raises an important question: are colleges and universities immune to the technological disruptions that have hit so many other sectors of the economy?

We'll take up that question in the next chapter.

8

Getting Down to Business: Why Abundance in Access and Instruction Hasn't Changed Higher Education

If you're like many of the people in academia I've talked to while working on this book, you probably feel at a gut level that colleges and universities are a special case—that they're somehow immune from the technological disruptions that have taken place in so many other sectors of the economy. And you probably feel this because you believe, deep down, that academia can't be thought of as a business. We're bigger and better than that. We have a grander mission. We don't merely offer a product for sale, and our students are not merely customers—or, as the factory model suggests, products.

This view is deeply—and, in many ways, rightly—embedded into the ethos of higher education. Writing in the *Chronicle of Higher Education* in a 2014 article titled "Faculty Members Are Not Cashiers," David Perry of the University of Minnesota summed up the way a lot of people feel about this question. "Students who believe that they are mere customers are selling themselves short," he declared, "as are the faculty members and administrators who apply business-speak to the classroom. . . . The responsibility of a teacher to his or her students is far greater than the employee to the customer."[1]

I completely agree. As educators, we have to hold ourselves to a higher standard of service to our students than what is implied by the term *customer*. Likewise, we have to hold ourselves to a higher standard of serving society than what is expected of profit-seeking enterprises. Our highest goal should always be to serve the needs of students in a way that benefits them individually and contributes to the broader social good.

But getting to your destination starts with an honest assessment of where you are. And for educators, that means acknowledging that there are many ways that our system of higher education *is* designed to run like a business—in ways that impede our ability to fully serve our students and society.

When we're being brutally honest, we actually admit that. Consider what the president of an elite university reportedly told a local community group in a talk titled "Why Does It Cost $60,000 a Year to Attend My University?"

The president provided three answers to that question. First, he said, even though technology has lowered prices in many other sectors of the economy, technology doesn't lower the cost of educating students. It actually raises them because, in addition to maintaining the existing physical plant and faculty salaries, the university now has to invest in hardware, software systems, and support staff, all of which are expensive.

Then he raised the arms-race problem. In a competitive market, when everyone else in higher education is spending hundreds of millions of dollars on new classrooms and fancy new dorms, his university has to match that spending if it wants to remain attractive to prospective students.

Neither of those reasons came as much of a surprise to the president's audience. But the third reason surely did, if only for its radical candor. Why charge students $60,000 a year to attend his university? "Because," the president said, "I fucking can!"

That's not the kind of language you hear often from a university president. But there's truth in it. The president went on to explain that even though his university, like so many others, regularly raises its tuition, students continue to apply in about the same numbers—which means that a lot of them are not price-sensitive. And as any economist will tell you, if your customers are willing to pay more, and if everyone else is charging more, then you should too. Indeed, when you are selling a product where quality is signaled by exclusivity, you almost have to.

In short, like it or not, given the way our existing system of higher education works, high-level university administrators often have to think about what they do in business terms. That's what happened not long ago at a major state university after the state's legislature capped the number of out-of-state students who could be admitted to the university. The state representatives were being perfectly reasonable given their responsibility to serve the needs of their state's taxpayers. But the decision created a revenue problem for the university because the tuition for out-of-state students was three times higher than the tuition for in-state students.

To solve this revenue problem, a high-level administrator at the university told me, the president and the provost decided to maximize the profitability of their out-of-state students by making sure that they or their families were wealthy enough not to need much financial aid. How did they do that? By using the same database marketing software used by for-profit firms and targeting the university's promotional materials to out-of-state students who live in high-income zip codes. In doing this, they excluded deserving lower-income students, which was a violation of their higher mission, but they had a revenue problem, and they solved it in the only way that the system allowed.

There are plenty of other examples—the amount of money colleges and universities spend on coaches and athletic facilities for "revenue-generating sports"; the willingness of university administrators to boost their bottom line by outsourcing their online educational programs to for-profit firms;[2] the willingness of some colleges to pay commissions of $1,000 to $1,600 to independent agents to increase enrollment from international students, who generally pay full tuition;[3] the collusion that seems to have taken place among elite colleges to limit the amount of financial aid they offer to admitted students in an effort to avoid getting into costly bidding wars for talent.[4] Behaviors like these prompted this tweet from George Siemens, a professor at the University of Texas at Arlington who also serves as the executive director of the university's Learning Innovation and Networked Knowledge Research Lab:

> I no longer think there's a huge difference between for-profit and public higher education. Sit in enough faculty meetings, meet with enough leadership, and it becomes clear that it's all about money. The difference between for-profit and public is mainly about appearances. In public institutions, we claim the higher ground but almost everything is driven by student numbers, enrollment, and dollars. Education could be less expensive, it could be more engaging, it could have a bigger impact, but we are confined to a system that values dollars first.[5]

Then there's the strong *external* perception that higher education is a business. When I talk to people outside the academy and tell them that many of my colleagues don't think of higher education as a business, they frequently laugh out loud. This is particularly true among parents who are taking out a second mortgage to put their kids through college, or students who are struggling to pay off their student loans. I admit that as a parent of three children in college, there are times I feel this way myself. On campus, in my role as a professor, I desperately want to believe that higher education is engaged in a noble mission to serve the interests of students and society. But when I come home and find my mailbox full of fancy promotional materials from colleges advertising their lavish facilities and consistent return on investment for graduates, and when I find myself writing five-figure checks to pay the invoices and late fees charged by my kids' universities, it sure feels like we are engaged in a business transaction.

By now, if I've done my job right so far in this book, maybe you're ready to concede that, whether we're aware of it or not, our current system of higher education functions as a business at least on some important dimensions. Students and their families accept that they're paying for a product and expect it be useful and worth the cost, and colleges and universities accept that they're selling that product and that they need to make money in order to remain relevant, viable, and competitive.

But even if you've come with me up to this point, you might still object, very reasonably, that higher education seems nonetheless to have eluded the kinds of market disruptions that have transformed other sectors of the economy in the past couple of decades. A decade ago, as I note briefly in chapter 7, lots of people were loudly heralding the imminent demise of our system of higher education thanks to the arrival of digital technology and the online instruction it made possible. But clearly that hasn't happened.

So what's going on? Is there something about higher education that somehow makes it immune to disruption after all?

*   *   *

Well, yes and no.

To understand why I'm hedging, we're going to have to wander briefly into the world of management theory. In particular, we're going to take a careful look at the trendy term *disruption*, which I've used a fair bit already in this book and which you've surely encountered in a variety of contexts, even if you have no interest or experience in business at all. What does the term mean, and how might it apply to higher education?

The person who made disruption famous about twenty-five years ago was the late Clay Christensen, a Harvard Business School professor who came to be known as the father of disruptive change theory. Christensen's pathbreaking research started, as pathbreaking research almost always starts, with a simple question. While most management scholars of his day were asking what causes some businesses to remain successful year after year, Christensen began wondering about something quite different: what causes some successful businesses to suddenly fail?

After giving this question some thought, Christensen zeroed in on the idea of disruptive change, an idea that he defined and put on the map in 1995 in a *Harvard Business Review* article titled "Disruptive Technologies." One of the main ways firms fail, Christensen suggested in the article, is that they pay *too much* attention to the needs of their existing customers.[6]

That's a paradoxical idea, and to make sense of it, we need a little more context. It's important to understand that in his article Christensen differentiated between innovations that were "sustaining" and those that were "disruptive."

Sustaining innovations, Christensen wrote, are made possible by new technologies that help companies deliver more value to existing customers, according to a well-understood set of needs. Customers are always looking for faster, higher-capacity hard drives in their computers, he noted, and the consistently successful companies in the industry tend to be those that constantly seek out and embrace new technologies that might help them sustain their advantage on that front.

Disruptive innovations, Christensen argued, are different. They don't deliver more value to a company's existing customers. In fact, they appear to offer *less*. That's what happened when new technologies made smaller hard drives possible. Initially, the drives were slower and lower-capacity than existing hard drives, so incumbent companies paid them little heed. They knew their customers wanted more speed and capacity, and these new drives offered neither, so they left the development of these smaller drives to new companies, figuring that they would be serving a different, less profitable market.

That's a perfectly sensible decision to make. The problem is, the technology that enabled the innovation often improves so rapidly that soon it *does* meet the needs of existing customers. At that point, the innovation can become more attractive than the old product, particularly when the innovation has additional advantages—in the case of hard drives, their smaller size. When that happens, the entrants that have invested in the new technology have a big jump on the incumbents, many of whom can never catch up. The industry has been disrupted.

Christensen's ideas caught on. Soon they were being applied in all sorts of arenas, and he himself even applied them to higher education. New forms of online education provided new sources of value at a far lower cost, he felt, and these new sources of value didn't appeal to existing customers who were accustomed to the "high-quality" residential-college experience. That made him feel that higher education was an industry ripe for disruption.

But the promised end hasn't come, so it's fair to wonder why Christensen got it wrong. Is it because the traditionalists are right, and higher education really can't be thought of as a business? Many people feel that's the case—but I fear they're not taking a broad enough view. In his work on disruption, Christensen focused on just one way that companies can lose power and influence by failing to perceive the threat posed by a significant change in its market environment. His work provides a great framework for understanding some forms of disruption—but it doesn't explain all of them.[7] You don't have to look hard, in fact, to find other situations where Christensen and his followers appear to have gotten things badly wrong.

In 2007, for example, Christensen identified the iPhone as a sustaining rather than a disruptive technology and, as a result, concluded that its "probability of success is going to be limited."[8] Nokia, he felt, need not be concerned.

Similarly, in 2015, Christensen dismissed the threat that Uber posed to the taxi industry. "Uber is clearly transforming the taxi business in the United States," he wrote. "But is it disrupting the taxi business? According to the theory, the answer is no."[9]

Also in 2015, Tom Bartman, a research associate of Christensen's, dismissed the threat Tesla posed to traditional car manufacturers. "Tesla is not a disrupter," he argued. Instead, he continued, it represented a "classic" case of sustaining innovation, in that what it really offered was "incrementally better performance at a higher price."[10]

Even if you don't follow or care much about business, you surely know how things panned out in each of these cases: the iPhone disrupted an industry that had been dominated by Nokia, Uber disrupted an industry that had been dominated by traditional taxi cabs, and Tesla disrupted market power in the auto industry. After a short period of denial, the incumbent firms recognized the threat that these companies and their innovative technologies posed to their business, but by that time, they had lost their advantage and have struggled to respond.

*   *   *

With all of this in mind, and with our eyes ultimately still on higher education, let's now explore a different type of disruption—one that in 2016, in the *Harvard Business Review*, the management scholar Joshua Gans, building on the research of Rebecca Henderson, a professor at Harvard Business School, formally identified as "supply-side disruption."[11]

In his article, Gans argues that Christensen had theorized only about the kinds of disruption that occur on the demand side of the market—as happens when firms underestimate how rapidly a new technology will develop to meet the needs of their customers. But Gans notes that disruption can also occur on the supply side—and that it works very differently there. Supply-side disruption occurs, he wrote, when incumbent firms recognize that new technologies pose threats to their business, but they nonetheless lack the capacity to respond—for the simple reason that they aren't able to "fundamentally change the way they manufacture and distribute their products."

To compete with the iPhone, Nokia realized early on, it would have to make a lot of changes. It would have to fundamentally redesign how it made its phones; it would have to make significant investments in touchscreen technology, which it had very little experience with; it would have to make significant investments in consumer software and operating system development; and it would have to make significant investments in the development of associated assets that could create lock-in to its newly broadened hardware ecosystem. In short, to respond to Apple's iPhone, Nokia would have to become like Apple—an enormously daunting and expensive undertaking. And that wasn't all. Nokia's executives also realized that if they transformed their business to better compete with Apple, they would threaten their existing fiefdoms and power. Understandably, they balked.

History is littered with examples of supply-side disruption. Similar arguments could be made regarding the *Encyclopaedia Britannica*'s inability to respond to the appearance of Microsoft Encarta in the late 1980s, and Microsoft's costly delay in responding to the iPad (another Apple innovation dismissed by Christensen) in the early 2010s.[12] In each case, the incumbent firm saw the threat posed by the new technology but was unable to respond because of the prohibitive cost of the necessary investment, and because of objections from powerful stakeholders. The sales representatives in the case of *Britannica*,[13] for example, didn't like the idea of losing the big commissions they earned for selling expensive printed encyclopedias, and executives in the powerful Windows and Office divisions of Microsoft worried that a tablet interface would undermine the value of their PC software products.[14]

A similar argument could be made for Yellow Cab and other incumbent taxi companies that, to compete effectively with Uber, would have had to abandon their investments in their existing fleets of cars (hurting the careers of the powerful people who were in charge of them) and instead make new investments in running a global software platform, a technology they had no experience with. Not surprisingly, they balked too.

That's also what General Motors and many incumbent automakers did initially when faced with the threat that Tesla posed to them. It's not hard to understand why they behaved this way. Embracing the production of electric vehicles would be risky for their established dealership model—where most of the money is made in not sales but service and where dealers would recognize that electric vehicles require far less service than gas-powered ones. A lot of people at the corporate level also found the idea of embracing electric vehicle technology unpalatable, for some pretty good reasons: it threatened the careers of powerful internal stakeholders, required massive new investments in new battery technologies and new factories, and invited difficult negotiations with unions concerning the retraining of existing factory workers.[15] So, once again, the companies balked, and now they are playing catch-up to a company they never expected would pose a threat.

*   *   *

So how might all of this arcane theory, broadened to include both the demand and supply sides, apply to the world of higher education?

I think it can teach those of us in higher education three key lessons about the threat that disruption may pose to us. First, it teaches us not to assume that we're immune to disruption just because the predictions of Clay Christensen and others haven't panned out. That's the mistake I believe Justin Reich makes in his 2020 book *Failure to Disrupt: Why Technology Alone Can't Transform Education*, which is focused on debunking Christensen but doesn't take supply-side disruption into account at all.[16]

Second, it teaches us not to assume that we're immune just because we're nonprofit institutions. That's the mistake I believe the Harvard historian Jill Lepore made in 2014 in a widely circulated *New Yorker* article. Lepore dismissed the relevance of Christensen and disruption theory to higher education because, as she put it, our "values and goals are remote from the values and goals of business."[17] Lepore did argue convincingly that Christensen's theory has been applied without sufficient empirical scrutiny, and far too broadly, but I can't accept her argument that we should dismiss outright the threat that disruption poses. Can we in higher education really dismiss the transformative power of digital technologies, which are so evident in every other sector of the economy, and trust that our "values and goals" will sustain us? I don't think so. Indeed, I hope I've made clear in this chapter that disruption doesn't require a profit motive: all it needs are self-interested human beings who shortsightedly oppose innovative technological change because it might undermine their power.

Third, what we've been discussing in this chapter can help us resist the analogy that some scholars have made between higher education and luxury goods. This is the approach taken by Michael Lanford and William Tierney, who, in their 2022 book *Creating a Culture of Mindful Innovation in Higher Education*, argue that higher education will survive the disruption predicted by Christensen in the very same way that the manufacturers of luxury mechanical watches have survived the disruption introduced by digital technologies.[18] One could ask whether, given our higher calling to serve students and society, we in higher education should be comfortable comparing ourselves to the producers of expensive Swiss watches and similar luxury goods. But for now, let's focus on the fact that an industry can be disrupted even if it isn't completely destroyed. Yes, a small number of high-end watch manufacturers are thriving in the presence of cheaper digital timekeeping technologies, but the cheaper alternatives have certainly disrupted power in the overall market. In the same way that Rolex, Cartier, and Patek Philippe are thriving in an age of disruptive digital timekeeping, Harvard, MIT, and Stanford will almost surely continue to thrive in a world of disruptive digital education. But even they face the prospect of serving a tiny niche market when the real action will be elsewhere.

*   *   *

So what actually *could* bring about disruption in higher education?

That's a vitally important question for universities, parents, students, and society—and it's why I've spent much of this chapter wandering about in the world of disruption theory. We're now prepared to discuss what I call *structural disruption*, which operates on both the demand and supply sides of markets and affects all sources of a firm's competitive advantage. This is the form of disruption that I think is about to shake up the world of higher education. We'll take it up in the next chapter.

9
Structural Disruption: Why Big Changes Are at Last on the Horizon for Higher Education

To understand why higher education is at last headed for a major disruption, we need to think about two important areas in which digital technology has already been transformative for other industries—scale and data.

Let's start with scale. Consider the situation in the entertainment industry. It costs several dollars to print and ship books, CDs, and DVDs, which means that there's no way to serve customers for whom the value of the product is less than the cost of printing and shipping. Those customers are automatically excluded from the market. But when products are digital, the cost of replicating and delivering the products drops to zero. In the digital world—as long as companies are selling at scale—it's possible to profitably serve any customer for whom the value of the product is greater than zero, and the result is market abundance in the form of low-priced digital subscription services. Think about how many CDs or vinyl records people used to own, and how much their collection would have cost, and compare that to how much music *anybody* who pays $10 a month to a streaming service can now have at their fingertips. As we business-school types like to say, digitizing the product has increased the competitive importance of scale.[1]

But digitization has also increased the competitive importance of data. When the product is digital, firms can see what people consume, for how long, how frequently, in what context, and so on. And they can then use that data to generate value for consumers by customizing the products they show to each individual customer and, in some cases, customizing the product itself to meet the needs of individual consumers. By collecting, analyzing, and using this data, Spotify can automatically recommend new artists for users, build playlists designed for an individual user's musical tastes, and create its popular year-end "wrap" for sharing with friends.

As all of this started to happen to the entertainment industry in the early 2000s, my colleagues and I followed these developments with great interest. We expected to start seeing significant changes pretty quickly, but we were surprised to discover that, at least initially, most established music labels, publishers, and motion picture studios weren't focused on making the most of new digital technologies to deliver their products to consumers in new ways. Instead, we saw them trying to use digital technologies in ways that conformed to how they'd always done business in a physical world. They were trying to figure out when to release e-books in their established hardcover and paperback release windows, how to price digital music in the context of their established CD prices, and how long to wait after broadcast before selling their television shows online. In all of this, they adopted a defensive posture: if they had to embrace new digital technologies, they wanted to do it without damaging their existing products and processes.

That was understandable, but, as my colleague Rahul Telang and I began to realize, it meant that they weren't focusing on the strategic threat that these new technologies represented to their businesses, and the ways they should respond to that threat. Most executives seemed to be telling themselves, "We'll be fine." Wave after wave of technological changes had hit their industries during the previous century, after all, and they'd always adapted successfully and retained their market dominance.

That's the attitude we encountered in 2015, when the president of home entertainment at a major motion picture studio came to our class at Carnegie Mellon University to talk about how technology was changing his business. After the executive wrapped up his talk, Rahul asked if he was at all concerned about the threat that Amazon, Google, and Netflix posed to his business. The executive was not. "The original players in this industry have been around for the last hundred years," he said, dismissively, "and there's a reason for that."

We knew why he felt that way. If you're part of an industry that's been around for a century without fundamental disruption to its model, then it's natural to believe that your industry has things figured out when it comes to the advent of new technologies. So you domesticate them to serve your present needs and allow you to preserve the status quo.

So why might today's technological shifts be any different?

That's the question Rahul and I set out to answer for the entertainment industry. In our 2016 book *Streaming, Sharing, Stealing: Big Data and the Future of Entertainment*, we examined how the likes of Amazon, Apple, Netflix, Spotify, and others were dramatically transforming the entertainment industry, and we tried to explain why so many executives at the traditionally dominant firms were blind to what was happening.[2]

Initially, we thought we'd be able to explain everything in the context of demand-side and supply-side theories of disruption. But we quickly discovered that these theories couldn't capture the full scope of the transformation that was under way in the industry. That's because these theories assumed a *single* technological shift, whereas the entertainment industry was facing at least five simultaneous shifts—the rise of distribution channels that allowed anyone, anywhere to access a global audience of potential consumers; the rise of distribution platforms that wielded far more market power than traditional brick-and-mortar retailers; the rise of detailed consumer-level data that created new ways to generate consumer value (and market power) for the firms that owned that data; the rise of digital piracy, which fundamentally changed the profitability of the industry's traditional sales channels; and the rise of user-generated content, fueled by high-definition cell phone video cameras and affordable editing software.

Each of these shifts was meaningful, but none on its own had the power to disrupt the industry landscape, either on the demand or the supply side. So traditional executives can be forgiven for feeling that they weren't under threat. The problem was that they weren't worrying about the fundamental threat that all of these shifts posed to their market power in the aggregate, at the same time. Let's call that the threat of *structural disruption.*

Structural disruption is the kind of threat that blindsided many players in the entertainment industry in the early 2000s, and it's the threat we face in higher education today.

*   *   *

The parallels are eerie.

A lot of people today are making claims about higher education that sound just like the claims that our class visitor and others in the entertainment industry were making a decade ago: "We'll be fine. We've been around for a long time, and we know what we're doing. Our model makes us immune to disruption. Decade after decade, we've survived by domesticating new technologies and neutralizing the threat that they pose to us. We just need to stay the course."

Because of these parallels, if you want something of a preview of how digital technology is likely to disrupt higher education, you can look back at how it disrupted the entertainment industry just a decade ago. But before doing that, let's set out a working definition. Structural disruption is what happens when multiple technological shifts converge to disrupt each of the sources of market power that previously had allowed a firm to thrive and maintain its market leadership. Those sources of power tend to involve the control of scarce resources, but in a structural disruption, *all* those resources become abundant, and then a new set of scarce resources becomes the source of market power— one that the traditional big players no longer control.

Think about how this played out in the entertainment industry. For decades, the same studios, labels, and publishers dominated their respective industries because they controlled three main scarcities—a scarcity in how content was created, a scarcity in how it was distributed, and a scarcity (granted via copyright law) in how it was consumed.

In the early 2000s, new digital technologies made a variety of changes possible. None of these was existentially threatening on its own, which gave executives a false sense of security. But collectively, these changes disrupted all of the aspects of firm power in the industry. They enabled user-generated content, which weakened the majors' ability to control scarcity in how content was produced. They created long tail markets, which weakened the majors' ability to control scarcity in how content was distributed. And they opened the door to digital piracy, which weakened the majors' ability to control scarcity in how content was consumed. At the same time, they created a new scarce and valuable resource—customer attention. What matters now in the structurally disrupted world of entertainment is the ability to gain control of the scarce data that allows you to understand your customer's preferences and desires at a detailed level, and the ability to design highly scalable processes and platforms that allow you to customize your offerings to serve each customer's unique needs.

With that in mind, let's now turn to higher education. But first let me note for the record that in comparing the stories of entertainment and higher education, in no way am I trying to suggest that these two industries are or should be the same or that they have the same goals. All I'm hoping to do is make clear that for a very long time both operated using models that resisted disruption; that this history bred complacency, short-sightedness, and even arrogance among senior managers; and that both industries, whether they recognize it or not, have been exposed to the very real and transformative threat of structural disruption.

The story of structural disruption in the entertainment industry also helps explain why Clay Christensen got it wrong when applying his theories to higher education. His theory of disruption is brilliant. But in thinking about how digital technology might or might not disrupt the industry, Christensen focused on a single technological innovation, MOOCs, which, as you'll recall, many people in the early 2000s were predicting would remake the industry in a decade or two. When that didn't happen, many of my colleagues concluded that higher education must be immune to disruption.

I think that's the wrong conclusion to draw from all of this, although it's a bit misleading even to use the word "wrong."

From the perspective of demand-side disruption theory, it made sense to predict the imminent disruption of higher education. It's hard to fault Christensen for doing that. New digital channels were inferior to the established residential programs, it's true, but they offered new sources of value that would surely appeal to a different market segment, and at a much lower price. And traditional universities were likely to reject those channels because they didn't appeal to their core customers or fit within their existing high margins. The demand was there, and the supplier was not. Disruption seemed to be imminent.

But that prediction has yet to pan out, and, despite what many people within academia would have you believe, that's not because higher education is immune to technological disruption, or because education isn't a business, or because we in academia are somehow special. It's because not all of the scarcities that represent sources of power in the industry have yet been made abundant.

As we've discussed, power in higher education has traditionally derived from the control of three scarce resources—scarcities in *access*, *instruction*, and *credentials*. MOOCs and a lot of the early advances in digital technology did a great job of making access and instruction more abundant, but they didn't make credentials any more abundant. That's what Clay Christensen and so many others missed. When did we see a structural disruption in the entertainment industry? It happened only when *all* of the traditional sources of power were disrupted by new technology. We haven't yet had a structural disruption in higher education because credentials remain scarce.

Think about it. Even if you can now take a Coursera class to learn calculus, microeconomics, or accounting, almost nobody is going to take you seriously in the job market if that's *all* you've done. Writ large across society, that's a huge problem. According to a 2022 study by Opportunity@Work, a nonprofit social venture whose mission is to help workers without a college diploma move up in the workforce, more than thirty million Americans who have the skills or experience to earn higher salaries are being held back by the lack of a four-year degree.[3]

In the end, it's depressingly simple: a university degree is still the credential that matters most in the workforce today. And therein lies the rub. As long as you need a degree to get a good job, the university system is safe from disruption.

*   *   *

Things are changing, however. There are strong signs that in the world of credentialing, we're now moving from scarcity to abundance. And that, in turn, suggests that conditions are at last ripe for a structural disruption in higher education.

Many factors are converging. One important factor is that more and more workers are seeking opportunities for new learning so that they can adapt to rapidly changing jobs and a rapidly changing economy—or even so that they can make a career change. This trend is particularly apparent in the tech sector, where, as we've been hearing for many years, there are more positions than qualified applicants. Typically, these midcareer learners don't have the time or money to pursue a traditional residential degree program. For a long time and for a lot of people, that represented an almost insurmountable obstacle. But during the past decade, as is discussed in previous chapters, new technologies have provided an abundance of access and instruction, and, as a result, lifelong learners now have a great supply of learning opportunities available to them.

This trend affects not just employees but also businesses. When universities were the only places offering training for white-collar jobs, it made sense for white-collar employers to rely on universities for credentials. But as instruction has become abundantly available outside the university system, employers are discovering

that they need new ways of evaluating and credentialing employee skills.

Another factor that supports structural disruption is
an increased social awareness among employers who
want a more diverse workforce—because it's the right
thing to do socially, but also because it leads to a stronger, more creative, and more productive workforce.
More and more employers are recognizing that higher
education hasn't been able to supply them with anywhere near the diversity that they need. As Amanda
Cage, the president and CEO of the National Fund for
Workforce Solutions pointed out during a January 2022
Wall Street Journal panel on the future of education, "If
you are putting out a job description that has a bachelor's degree [requirement], you are automatically elimi-
nating 68 percent of African Americans, 79 percent of
Latinx people in this country, 73 percent of rural Americans, and two-thirds of our nation's veterans."[4]

With all of these factors converging, a new market for
education and credentials has begun to emerge—and
some forward-looking employers have even decided to
bypass higher education altogether and jump into the
game themselves. This shift has been well documented.
In 2022, for example, Joseph Fuller, Christina Langer,
and Matt Sigelman reported in the *Harvard Business
Review* that in the world of training and hiring, a "structural reset" is under way. Their description of the situation is worth quoting at some length:

> If demand for talent far outreaches supply, employers
> de-emphasize degrees. That became increasingly
> apparent during the tight employment market of the
> late 2010s. Between 2017 and 2019, employers reduced
> degree requirements for 46% of middle-skill positions
> and 31% of high-skill positions. Among the jobs most
> affected were those in IT and managerial occupations,
> which were hard to fill during that period.
>
> The essence of the structural reset is this: In
> evaluating job applicants, employers are suspending
> the use of degree completion as a proxy and instead
> now favor hiring on the basis of demonstrated skills
> and competencies. This shift to skills-based hiring
> will open opportunities to a large population of
> potential employees who in recent years have often
> been excluded from consideration because of degree
> inflation.[5]

As the authors of this article acknowledge, the current shift to skills-based hiring is most apparent when it comes to "trade" skills such as programming, data analytics, business, engineering, and product design—skills that some higher education insiders derisively call "the servile arts." Call them what you will, but the need for these skills makes up a significant part of the demand for higher education today, and a significant part of the promotional messaging that universities use to entice students to apply. If new credentials reduce demand for degrees that provide these skills, soon many universities aren't going to have enough customers to meet their fixed costs of operation. That's a market reality we need to face.

And here's another reality we need to face: an increasing number of people no longer even *want* university credentials. "For the first time in my lifetime," Harvard's president, Lawrence Bacow, observed in 2018 in his inaugural address, "people are actually questioning the value of sending a child to college. For the first time in my lifetime, people are asking whether or not colleges and universities are worthy of public support. For the first time in my lifetime, people are expressing doubts about whether colleges and universities are even good for the nation. These questions force us to ask: What does higher education really contribute to the national life?"[6]

Most leaders in higher education aren't nearly as willing as Bacow to face up to the facts. According to a 2014 Gallup survey cited in the preface, 96 percent of chief academic officers at institutions of higher education institutions say their institution is "very or somewhat" effective at preparing students for the world of work, but only 14 percent of Americans—and 11 percent of business leaders—strongly agree with that statement.[7]

There is one more parallel here with what happened in the entertainment industry that's worth mentioning. For a long time, cable television executives assumed that people were thrilled with their service because they were willing to pay bloated prices for what was widely agreed to be an inferior product. But during the past ten years, it's become clear that customers weren't paying for cable TV because they loved it. They were paying because it was their only option. As soon as other options became available, cable TV customers cut the cord in droves.

Everything I've heard from students and parents as I've researched this book suggests we're in a very similar position in higher education today. Colleges and universities have for decades maintained a kind of monopoly control over credentialing, which has meant that students and their families feel that they have no choice but to buy into the system, no matter what it costs. And this, in turn, has made the industry seem impervious to disruption.

But colleges and universities may at last be losing their hold on credentialing. If that's true, what kind of changes might we start to see, and what would it mean for us as a society?

We'll tackle those questions in the next chapter.

10
Hello, Google State: The New World of Credentialing and Skills-Based Hiring

In chapter 5, we discussed how much of the value of a university degree comes from the signal it sends to the job market. That's because, in the absence of detailed information about an applicant's skills and motivation, employers are forced to rely on weak signals—whether the applicant was willing and able to complete a college degree, for example, and which university awarded that degree.

The branding signal sent by a university degree is good because it helps hiring managers evaluate talent. But it also can be bad because it encourages universities to do whatever it takes to boost and protect their brand. It also encourages employers to ignore qualified applicants simply because those applicants didn't have the opportunity or resources to complete a degree.

Can we do better? What if in many situations we could reliably separate an individual's true knowledge and skills from the weak signal conferred by university credentials? Could that diminish some of the harms created by our current credentialing system? And wouldn't that, in effect, help us get rid of the last remaining scarcity in higher education—the scarcity of credentials—which still holds so many people back, both socially and economically?

We're closer to this new reality than you might think. As noted in the previous chapter, when access to instruction was scarce, it made perfect sense for employers to rely on university degrees when making hiring decisions. How else could they be sure that applicants had the advanced skills they needed to do the jobs they were applying for? But, as we've seen, two of the three main scarcities in higher education, access and instruction, are now becoming abundantly available, which means it's far easier today than ever before for learners to gain knowledge outside of a traditional university environment. Given that, maybe it's time for employers to evaluate job applicants' qualifications based on their true knowledge and skills rather than the brand name of the university listed on their résumé.

The shift I'm arguing for here is similar to shifts that have already occurred in other areas of the economy. For a long time, if you needed to decide what product to buy, what restaurant to visit, or where to stay, you had to rely on the weak signals conferred by brand name. But now, reputation platforms like Airbnb, Amazon, Trip Advisor, and Yelp provide rankings and ratings for goods and services in ways that have significantly reduced the value of traditional brand names in many markets.[1]

To many traditionalists in the academy, hiring people based on their online reputation rather than their university credentials might seem like a crazy idea. But this isn't as far-fetched as it might sound. Consider that in 2015, the hottest data science recruit in Silicon Valley was Gilberto Titericz, a petroleum engineer with a degree from the thirteenth-best university in Brazil and who was working at Petrobas, Brazil's state oil company. Why were tech firms interested in Titericz? Not because of his university's brand, which was nothing special; his undergraduate major, which was unrelated; or his work experience, which was limited and irrelevant. They were attracted by a new kind of signal—the top ranking that Titericz had earned on the data science leaderboard at a company called Kaggle.[2]

Kaggle is a big deal. The company hosts an online community of about 500,000 data science enthusiasts, and its mission is to connect them with companies and government agencies around the world that need data analytics problems solved. Companies post data sets and questions related to their problems on Kaggle, and members of the community are then free to work on anything that interests them. Sometimes companies offer significant amounts of prize money. Zillow recently sponsored a $1.2 million competition that was designed to help the company improve its home-value prediction algorithms,[3] and a $1.5 million competition sponsored by the Department of Homeland

Security was designed to improve the department's threat-recognition algorithms.[4]

Given the size of the online community at Kaggle, you have to be *really* good at what you do to excel in these competitions, and if you do, then you'll start rising up on the leaderboards that the company maintains. Employers have started to pay attention to these leaderboards because of the quality of the signal they send about the skills of the people on them—a signal that, in many ways, is stronger and clearer than that sent by a university degree. Some companies have even started to include involvement in Kaggle competitions as a requirement for their data analytics jobs. When Intel recently posted an announcement for the role of deep-learning engineer, for example, it listed as a minimum qualification "experience with participating in and winning Kaggle competitions."[5]

That's exactly the kind of experience that made Gilberto Titericz such a hot commodity. While working at Petrobas, he spent nights teaching himself about data analytics online, and learning from the advice available in Kaggle's online community discussion boards. He then put his skills to use on Kaggle, where he quickly rose to the top of the data science leaderboard. And once he got there, he soon received job offers from Tesla and Google—and Airbnb, where he now works.

Other companies are doing much the same thing. Sites such as CrowdAI, Google's Code Jam, HackerRank, and Topcoder are all making names for themselves as places where companies can find top-quality coders and data scientists—so much so, in fact, that many leading technology firms now give more weight to job applicants' rankings on these platforms than to their university credentials. This is a natural extension of the democratizing power of the internet and digital technologies, which in the past couple of decades have made it much more possible for people without formal credentials or associations to make their skills known in the world of work. Think, for example, of how Twitter and Substack have helped writers find audiences and publishers find writers.

But companies don't have to rely solely on third parties to evaluate job applicants. They can also do it themselves—increasingly, again, in ways that undermine the value of a traditional university degree. That's what's happening at Google. After analyzing employee data, the company discovered that applicants' GPAs and college test scores were almost useless for predicting whether they would succeed at Google. So now, instead of relying on college transcripts to evaluate talent, Google relies on a series of practical tests and behavioral interviews, a shift that has led the company to hire substantially more employees without college degrees.[6]

LinkedIn has adopted a similar approach to hiring. The company used to pride itself on recruiting from a very small group of elite universities, but then it took a close look at the performance of its employees and discovered that those who made "the biggest difference" were often those without traditional degrees. So the company has changed its approach. According to Jeff Wiener, the company's CEO, its new hiring focus is "skills not degrees."[7]

As we discussed in chapter 9, other organizations have already started to embrace that idea. In the years ahead, many more will surely join in—and as they do, we're going to see a lot of people realize that they don't need a traditional degree to become successful members of the professional workforce.

*   *   *

Another important change is under way: some companies have decided to educate and train employees themselves. What's emerging as a result—according to Sean Gallagher, the founder and executive director of Northeastern University's Center for the Future of Higher Education and Talent Strategy, and Holly Zanville, the codirector of the Program on Skills, Credentials & Workforce Policy at George Washington University's Institute of Public Policy—is an "employer-issued credentialing ecosystem" that has the potential to transform the landscape of higher education.[8]

Amazon established itself as a leader on this front in the summer of 2019, when it announced plans to spend $700 million to "upskill" 100,000 of its employees by 2025, readying them for new jobs not only at Amazon but elsewhere. That announcement, not surprisingly, caused consternation in the world of higher education. Less than a week later, in an article titled "Employers as

Educators," *Inside Higher Ed* described Amazon's move as "a shot across the bow for colleges and universities."[9]

The press release that Amazon put out at the time of its announcement makes clear why the company's announcement provoked this kind of reaction. The release describes several ambitious and nontraditional educational offerings:

> *Amazon Technical Academy*, which equips non-technical Amazon employees with the essential skills to transition into, and thrive in, software engineering careers;
>
> *Associate2Tech*, which trains fulfillment center associates to move into technical roles regardless of their previous IT experience;
>
> *Machine Learning University*, offering employees with technical backgrounds the opportunity to access machine learning skills via an on-site training program;
>
> *AmazonCareer Choice*, a pre-paid tuition program designed to train fulfillment center associates in high-demand occupations of their choice;
>
> *Amazon Apprenticeship*, a Department of Labor certified program that offers paid intensive classroom training and on-the-job apprenticeships with Amazon; and
>
> *AWS Training and Certification*, which provide employees with courses to build practical AWS Cloud knowledge that is essential to operating in a technical field.[10]

In the business world, what Amazon is doing in this move is called *vertical integration.* Amazon did much the same thing a decade or so ago in the realm of entertainment after discovering, along with Netflix, that the films and shows being produced for a mass-market audience by the Hollywood studios weren't well suited to the business of on-demand streaming. To ensure a steady supply of the kind of targeted binge-worthy series they needed, both Amazon and Netflix decided that they more or less *had* to start producing their own shows. So they did—and the rest is history. The shows they're now producing are winning all sorts of awards and attracting millions of viewers, and both companies have become dominant players in the entertainment business. Which makes you wonder: Given how successfully Amazon managed vertical integration in the world of entertainment, and given how serious it seems to be about getting into skills training, and given that Amazon is Amazon, does anybody doubt that big changes might be coming if the company tries to achieve a similar kind of dominance in the newly emergent credentialing ecosystem?

Amazon isn't the only company in this space. Google has recently launched Google Career Certificates, along with 100,000 scholarships. It's an effort that the company says will "help Americans get qualifications in high-paying high-growth job fields—no college degree required."[11] As is the case with Amazon, Google clearly feels that it can do better than traditional colleges and universities at giving tech workers the skills they need to succeed in the modern workplace. Ken Walker, Google's senior vice president of global affairs, recently made clear how seriously the company takes the Career Certificates program. For many roles, he said, "We will consider our new career certificates as the equivalent of a four-year degree."

Other companies are rushing to jump into the game. IBM, which recently committed itself to a similar skills-over-degrees approach to hiring, now runs a digital badging program for its employees that has awarded 3.7 million credentials to employees during the past seven years.[12] AT&T runs the enormously popular in-house credentialing program that it calls AT&T University. Microsoft has recently announced plans for a multi-million-dollar initiative that will provide digital skills training for twenty-five million people—a move that suggests the company sees great value in making training available to many more people that just its own employees. "Talent is everywhere but the opportunity is not," Satya Nadella, the company's CEO, said in announcing the initiative. "Over and over again, we see that when people have access to education and skilling, they create new opportunities for themselves and other people."[13]

This phenomenon isn't limited to technology jobs. SAP, for example, now runs a selective Sales Academy, which virtually guarantees account executive positions to successful students.[14] Jamie Dimon, the CEO of JP Morgan, not long ago declared that the new world of work is "about skills, not necessarily degrees," and he has committed real resources to this idea. The company has committed itself to putting $350 million into skills training conducted via "non-traditional career pathway programs."[15] Even companies as different as Koch Industries and Frito-Lay—neither of which can be described as a Silicon Valley pioneer—have launched their own credentialing and apprenticeship programs.[16]

Where things are going is clear, according to Catherine Ward, the managing director of private-sector strategies for JFFLabs, a division of the nonprofit group Jobs for the Future. "This is no fluke," Ward told *Inside Higher Ed* in 2019. "This is going to be happening more and more."[17]

Even some academics are starting to recognize the threat. For example, in a November 2020 article in the *Wall Street Journal*, Christopher Dede of Harvard's Graduate School of Education observed that "the minute you have enough groups from industry, or the military or nonprofits, validate these things, you provide a way of bypassing educational institutions, and that will open the door to people not having to get a bachelor's degree as a warrant to enter the workplace."[18]

*   *   *

It's notable that a good number of the companies I've discussed above have chosen to offer their credentialing programs in collaboration with traditional institutions of higher education.

Amazon Web Services, for example, announced in 2019 that it would work with George Mason University and Northern Virginia Community College to offer a bachelor's degree program in cloud computing. That plan grew out of Amazon's decision to locate its second headquarters in northern Virginia, where it will need a readily available supply of skilled workers—workers with the kinds of cutting-edge training that most colleges and universities aren't offering. "AWS identified the skills and competencies successful employees must have, and our faculty designed the courses," Michelle Marks, GMU's vice president for academic innovation and new ventures, told the press. "This new pathway demonstrates our commitment to creating both educational and employment access. These students will be prepared to compete for our region's most in-demand jobs."[19]

In a similar vein, Google has teamed up with Coursera to make its certificate program for IT support professionals widely available, and the program is already offered at a hundred community colleges around the country. *Inside Higher Ed* applauded the move when it was announced, praising Google for opting not "to compete with traditional institutions" but "to collaborate instead, potentially extending higher education's reach rather than threatening the degree."[20]

I'm not so sure I share that assessment. For now, these programs are collaborative and seem to be extending the reach of traditional institutions. But my guess, based on how these companies have operated in other domains, is that once they've figured out what works best, they'll gradually stop collaborating and strike out on their own, taking a lot of students with them.

I'm not the only one who has that feeling. In a white paper titled "It's Time to Transform Higher Education," for example, Jeff Brown, the dean of the Gies College of Business at the University of Illinois, recently expressed a similar idea, writing, "Many of our most valuable corporate partners—those who hire our students, provide philanthropic support, serve on our advisory boards, and speak to our classes—are becoming not only valuable collaborators but also potential competitors. Tech companies like Amazon, Apple, Google, and Microsoft are offering their own badges, certificates and credentials."[21]

That's probably why many people in traditional institutions of higher learning find this new world of credentialing so threatening. Consciously or unconsciously, they recognize that we're headed for a world in which an employee's knowledge and skills are increasingly separate from any kind of signal gained through holding a university credential. It's probably also why some elite colleges and universities are now starting to think in terms of not only degrees but also skills—and are starting to offer à la carte microcredentials alongside traditional four-year courses of study. This makes sense: they don't want to cede the rapidly growing credentialing market to the big corporate players. And there really are remarkable opportunities in this market for colleges and students alike. More than 40 percent of the people who start bachelor's degree programs today fail to finish within six years,[22] and right now there are some thirty-six million people in the workforce who have completed some college coursework without having anything to show for it.[23] Those are all people who presumably would be better off if they'd been able to earn valuable credentials along the way. Clark Gilbert, the president of BYU-Pathway Worldwide, which offers online degrees and microcredentials, certainly thinks so. "If we lose someone," Gilbert told *Wired* in 2020, "instead of being a dropout, they'll have a certificate. Is it as good as having a bachelor's degree? No, it's not. But is it better than being a dropout? Yes, it is."[24]

As with many of the other innovations discussed in this book, I'm not in any way arguing that the rise of credentialing will spell the end of the traditional college or university as we know it. There are plenty of fields of study, and plenty of kinds of employment, that don't lend themselves neatly to the kinds of signaling and credentialing that I've been talking about. Signaling your job qualifications through online reputation platforms or employer-sponsored credentialing programs will never be *for* everybody, nor should it be. But we'll be much better off as a society if we do everything we can to make those platforms and programs available *to* everybody, particularly the many individuals who otherwise wouldn't be able to pursue a degree—not because they lacked the talent but because they lacked the financial resources, time, or academic "pedigree" necessary to succeed in our current system.

To me, it's a no-brainer. With so many more options for skills training available, especially in technology-based work, and with so many companies becoming willing to hire based on skills rather than degrees, two very good things are likely to happen in the years ahead: lots of people will be trained and hired for skilled jobs that were previously inaccessible to them, and a decent number of students who previously would have gone to a four-year undergraduate program will decide that they can get the education and jobs they need without going hundreds of thousands of dollars into debt.

Like it or not, this really does seem to be in our future. Northeastern's Sean Gallagher has found that organizations have grown demonstrably more interested in skills- and competency-based hiring. In 2018, when Gallagher conducted a survey of 750 human resources leaders at US companies that spanned all industry sectors and organizational sizes, he found that a majority were either pursuing "a formal effort to deemphasize degrees and prioritize skills" or were at least actively exploring it.[25] And it's probably not coincidental that in recent years the proportion of US adults who believe college is very important has dropped dramatically.[26]

*   *   *

As someone who studies technological change in industries, I find this emerging reality terrifying . . . but also invigorating.

Why terrifying? For hundreds of years, market power in higher education has been defined by a university's ability to control scarcity in access, instruction, and credentials—but digital technologies are now making these scarce resources abundant. In every other industry I've studied, whenever the scarce resources that previously defined power in a market have become abundant, turmoil has ensued for the firms that previously held power. I don't see why higher education should be any different.

For those of us in academia, this raises all sorts of unsettling questions. As we get abundance in access, how many students will discover that online classes provide the knowledge they need—at a far lower price than a traditional residential university could ever provide? As we get abundance in instruction, will business schools still need the likes of tenured professors like me to explain the work of experts to our students when each of those experts could do it better—and at a lower cost—themselves? As we achieve abundance in outcomes, how many students will discover that they can signal their skills and potential to employers without the need to invest years in pricey university degrees? What would that outcome mean for universities? What would it mean for me and a lot of my colleagues?

Nobody relishes the prospect of obsolescence. But here's the thing: even though I'm terrified about what's to come, I also feel a great sense of optimism, opportunity, and responsibility. For hundreds of years, scarcities of access, instruction, and outcome in higher education have left behind talented, capable, and potentially productive members of society. If we can move beyond our fears and embrace the changes that new technologies and ideas are making possible, changes that I think will lead to a new era of educational abundance, then we'll be able to serve these people—and, ultimately, ourselves and our society—better. The big choice we face is this: will we resist these changes in the hopes of protecting our current model, or will we embrace them in the hopes of better fulfilling our mission and finally remedying some of the injustices created by the model that we've been a part of for so long?

I hope we'll do the latter, which is why I've written this book. Given what we know about the moral injustices of our current system, we in higher education should *want* to change—and, indeed, should recognize that we have a moral obligation to do so. It's time to get going on this project. And the first step is to analyze our reluctance.

11
Objections, Objections: Understanding and Moving Past Our Resistance to Change

As I worked on this book, I gave a lot of talks to university audiences on how technology can help us create a more just, affordable, and accessible system of higher education. I also had a lot of private discussions with colleagues. Throughout it all, I received a lot of pushback. The objections fall into four main categories, each of which is worth attending to.

The *first objection* is that online education can't compete with the quality of residential education. I've heard some variation of this objection in nearly every talk I've given. I don't think it's a persuasive one empirically, contextually, or ethically.

Let's start with the empirical problem with this objection. In advancing it, faculty tend to cite the inferior quality of education that teachers were able to deliver over Zoom during the COVID-19 lockdown. I generally agree with this take: in many cases, the Zoom education we offered students back in 2020 wasn't great, and in some cases, it may even have been disastrous. But is the quality of what we delivered during COVID the right reference point for judging the long-term potential of online education? In the spring of 2020, small groups of faculty members with no prior training in technology-enabled education suddenly had to make a complete pivot to online learning—in a month. Is it any surprise that they weren't able to produce a uniformly high-quality experience? Do we really believe that what they managed to do represents the full potential of online education? To me that sounds a little like deciding in the mid-1990s that there's no future for selling books online because independent booksellers' initial websites delivered only rudimentary search capabilities and had clunky payment processing.

Then there's the contextual problem with this objection. It's true that online learning didn't work for many of "our students"—that is, those who, because they had enrolled in our institutions, were already likely to prefer in-person education. But that doesn't mean remote education won't work for lots of other students. As we've discussed, there are many people out there who are unfairly excluded from our pricey time- and space-bound residential degrees who might benefit greatly from access to online education. Shouldn't we take their interests into account?

Finally, there's the ethical problem with this objection. If the online education we delivered during COVID really was inferior to the on-campus experience our students paid for, how much less valuable was it? Be as specific as you can.

When I put this question to skeptics, they tend to hem and haw at first. But eventually, when pressed for a number, they give me something in the 20 percent to 50 percent range. Fine. But if that's true, don't we have an obligation to give our students a tuition discount somewhere in that same range? When I've asked colleagues to explain to me why it was okay for their institution to charge full price for a product that they've just told me was substantially inferior, the most honest response I've heard was this: "Okay, yes, maybe we did knowingly overcharge our students during COVID. But what were we supposed to do? We had to keep the business running."

You could certainly turn the tables on me here and ask what *I'm* doing to ensure that my students at Carnegie Mellon will be getting a discount for the remote education they received during COVID. The answer is pretty simple. As I see it, the online education I delivered during COVID was worse—except for the parts that were better. And those parts include the ability for students to rewatch portions of classes that might not have made sense the first time; the ability to bring in high-quality guest speakers who didn't have the time to participate in-person; the flexibility to accommodate disruptions in student's schedules due to illness or other unexpected events; and the ability to use technology to create a sense of online community and encourage participation, particularly among students who might not have felt comfortable raising their hands in an in-person environment.[1] In my view, those things are worth a lot and make up for whatever value we lost in other ways.

The other reason I'd argue it was fair to keep our prices the same during COVID is that, to be blunt about it, I don't think most students are as concerned with the educational experience we offer them as they are with the value of the credential we provide. In the end, *that's* what they're paying us for. So as long as COVID didn't reduce the value of the credentials we offer them, there's an argument to be made that they still received what they signed up for.

*   *   *

I know that saying such a thing is tantamount to sacrilege in the world of liberal arts education, where the received wisdom—and the *second objection* to online learning—is that we don't need to change because our residential model of higher education is vitally important to students, employers, and society. When students take courses in history, literature, or philosophy with us, the theory goes, they develop transferable habits of critical thinking that will serve them—and all of us—well in both the workplace and society.

It's hard not to endorse that idea. But how true is it?

Not very, at least according to the economist Bryan Caplan of George Mason University. In *The Case against Education: Why the Education System Is a Waste of Time and Money* (2018), Caplan argues that there's surprisingly little evidence of a causal relationship between increased education and increased critical-thinking skills. As he puts it; "Educational psychologists who specialize in 'transfer of learning' have measured the hidden intellectual benefits of education for over a century. Their chief discovery: education is narrow. As a rule, students learn only the material you specifically teach them . . . if you're lucky."[2] A bit later, caustically, he adds, "Our education system rests on educators' conceit—the self-serving line that when we teach students whatever interests us, they durably acquire whatever skills they need to succeed in life."[3]

That line of thinking drives a lot of people who believe in the intangible value of the liberal arts crazy. It even rubs *me* the wrong way at times because I'll admit to being as attached as the next professor to the idea that what I teach has not only practical but also social value. But the problem, as I see it, is that regardless of what we tell ourselves as faculty, a lot of students and potential students just aren't interested in acquiring abstract skills of critical thinking that will help them become more informed members of the body politic. They're mainly interested in acquiring credentials that will get them a job. For example, according to surveys conducted by UCLA's Higher Education Research Institute in 2019, 84 percent of incoming college freshmen listed "to get a better job" as "very important" in their decision to go to college, compared with just 50 percent of incoming freshmen in 1975.[4] Americans, overall, seem to hold similar views. In a 2021 national survey sponsored by the Association of American Universities, two thousand adults were asked "how important is it, if at all, for a college or university to prioritize" a list of nine potential university initiatives. The initiative that came in at the top of the list was "Preparing students for future careers," with 92 percent of respondents listing it at very or somewhat important and 23 percent saying it was the single most important goal universities should prioritize.[5]

One could argue that these survey respondents are just narrowminded and shortsighted about the true value of a college education. Maybe so. But if that's true, we need to accept our culpability in encouraging those shortsighted views. After reading the promotional materials colleges have sent to my three children over the last six years, I've seen firsthand that—whatever my colleagues and I might believe about the broader personal and societal benefits of critical thinking skills and a liberal education—the way universities sell a college education to parents and students is based almost exclusively on plush campuses, luxury accommodations, and good-paying jobs.

I suspect these marketing messages aren't accidental. Rather, they're based on a careful understanding of what we know students and parents are looking for from the college degree. Whether or not we like it, a lot of students really *do* think of themselves as customers in search of a high-paying job. If they can find ways of acquiring credentials and finding a job that involve far less time and cost less money than the way we do things now, they're going to pursue them.

At this point, I'm frequently asked: "Wouldn't this be bad for society? Don't we need universities to produce informed citizens who can think critically and speak knowledgably about a broad variety of issues?"

It's perfectly reasonable to worry that society might suffer if we were to let go of the idea that everybody should be educated as broadly as possible in the liberal arts, ideally through a four-year residential experience. But in that case, you should be worrying about not only the benefits of that kind of educational experience but also its costs—the upwardly spiraling tuition rates, the crushing student-loan debt, the growing inequities in access, the widening class divide, and more. On balance, is it unreasonable to ask whether the benefits really outweigh all of those costs?

The other thing I think we should question is whether pricey residential degrees are the only way to create informed, socially minded citizens—a view many in higher education seem to hold. In 2012, for example, Cary Nelson, the outgoing president of the American Association of University Professors, had this to say about the dangers of online learning. "It's not education," he said, speaking to *Inside Higher Ed*, "and it's not even a reliable means for credentialing people." Instead, he suggested, it was best suited for people in retirement homes, "where folks are unlikely to assume any social responsibilities for the 'knowledge' they have acquired."[6]

I think we need to question that assumption. Is a residential college education the only way to prepare young adults—and lifelong learners, for that matter—to thrive in the world? Does preparation for the workforce really require four years of time on campus and hundreds of thousands of dollars of expense, and should it be disproportionately available to the wealthiest classes of society?

*   *   *

There's a strongly held view in higher education that whatever the inequalities created by our current system of higher education, online education will create even more. This *third objection* is an argument worth considering seriously.

Two articles published during the past decade in the journal *Science* seem to back up this claim. A 2019 article titled "The MOOC Pivot" analyzes data from students enrolled in all edX courses taught by MIT and Harvard from October 2012 through May 2018—and concludes that MOOCs have been a dismal failure at improving equity.[7] Why? Because 78 percent of the students who enrolled in Harvard and MIT's edX courses came from the world's most affluent countries and only 2 percent came from the world's least affluent countries as defined by the United Nations.[8] From this, the authors of the study conclude that MOOCs have failed at "creating new pathways at the margins of global higher education" and that "The 6-year saga of MOOCs provides a cautionary tale for education policymakers."

The fact that 78 percent of the students who took MIT and Harvard's edX classes came from highly developed countries and only 2 percent came from the world's least affluent countries certainly sounds like a damning critique of online education. But consider this: During that same period, 96 percent of the students who took classes on MIT and Harvard's physical campuses came from the world's most affluent countries, and only 0.3 percent came from the least affluent. Isn't that an even more dismal failure?

And these ratios tell only part of the story. When you look at the number of individuals in each ratio, you find that between 2014 and 2018, Harvard and MIT admitted a total of 423 students from the world's least affluent countries, whereas during that same period, HarvardX and MITx provided educational access to 192,223 students from the least affluent countries, among them Afghanistan, Chad, Haiti, Rwanda, Senegal, and Syria.

An earlier study, from 2015, titled "Democratizing Education?" draws a similar conclusion about the socioeconomic failures of online education.[9] In that study, the authors looked at sixty-eight MOOC courses offered by MIT and Harvard between 2012 and 2014 and found that MOOC participants "resided in neighborhoods where the median household income was $69,641 dollars, which was $11,998 dollars above the neighborhood national average of $57,643." This led the authors to conclude that "MOOCs and similar approaches to online learning can exacerbate . . . disparities in educational outcomes related to socioeconomic status."

Again, that sounds damning. But according to the *New York Times*, the students on Harvard's and MIT's physical campuses during this period came from families with, on average, household incomes of $137,400 and $168,000.[10] If attracting students from households making $12,000 more than the national average raises serious concerns about socioeconomic injustice, shouldn't we be even more worried about institutions that attract students from households that make $80,000 to $100,000 above the national average?[11]

It's important to recognize that these papers were written during a time where people were making bold claims that MOOCs were about to change everything, and in that context, maybe it made sense to point out that MOOCs are unlikely to create perfect equity. But that's not the real issue today, is it? To me, the question we should be asking isn't whether MOOCs will create perfectly equitable outcomes, as laudable as that goal might be. It's whether MOOCs and other educational technologies can create learning opportunities for students who otherwise would be left behind. And based on the data, the answer to that question is clearly yes.

Are MOOCs perfect? No. Are they different from in-person education? Of course. Would it be great if Harvard and MIT could provide affordable residential access to 200,000 students from the world's most impoverished countries? Yes, indeed.

But they can't. So we're left with a different set of questions and answers: Did MITx and HarvardX classes provide access to students who otherwise would have never been allowed access to MIT's and Harvard's classrooms? Absolutely. Do Harvard's and MIT's online courses reach a population that is far more socioeconomically diverse than the population served on these schools' physical campuses? Undoubtedly. And most important: Is this service valuable to the students who receive it?

The students seem to think so, at least according to survey results published in 2015 on the *Harvard Business Review* website. "MOOCs do have a real impact," the article states: "72% of survey respondents reported career benefits and 61% reported educational benefits. . . . In developed countries, career builders with low socioeconomic status and lower levels of education report tangible career benefits at about the same rate as those with high status and lots of education. And in developing countries, those with lower levels of socioeconomic status and education are significantly more likely to report tangible career benefits."[12]

We in higher education should be thrilled about this, and we should actively be looking to make outcomes for online learners even better. But on the whole, we aren't. Instead, we're digging in our feet and resisting.

*   *   *

This brings us to the *fourth objection* I've commonly heard about online education: no one can force us to change. After Clay Christensen's keynote address at the

2014 "Innovation and Disruption in Higher Education" conference at Colgate University, there was a lively panel discussion. During that discussion, Joan Hinde Stewart, the president of Hamilton College, said she disagreed with Christensen's conclusions about the future of higher education because, as she put it, "universities have been around for a very, very long time . . . because they are fundamentally conservative institutions."[13]

Stewart was right to say that colleges are among the most conservative of our social institutions, at least when it comes to adopting change. But an inability or unwillingness to change isn't a defense against disruption. Indeed, as we showed in chapter 8, these qualities can make you *more* vulnerable to disruption.

I believe Stewart was also wrong in assuming that our conservatism is something innate and immutable rather than an intentional choice. To see why, let's start by noting that describing universities as "fundamentally conservative institutions" sounds odd at first. We in higher education think of ourselves as progressive when it comes to change. Most academics look at conservatives as "the other people"—you know, the sort who are willing to cling to an outdated way of doing things because the old way benefits their privileged position in society.

Still, it's worth wondering if the shoe fits. Is there an argument to be made that part of the reason higher education hasn't been disrupted by technology is that "conservative" faculty are actively standing in the way of technological change?

Consider this story. On May 7, 2013, Dean Michael D. Smith (yes, the other Michael D. Smith) explained to the Harvard Faculty of Arts and Sciences why the university had chosen to participate in the edX online platform. "The world is moving in this way," he said, "and we should be part of this conversation because we are looked at as a leader in higher education."[14]

Not everybody was convinced. Charles S. Maier, a professor of history, voiced a common concern. "These things may be taking place in the world," he said, "but my own sense is that there is a great fast train at the station, and we're rushing to get on without knowing where it is going." Two weeks later, fifty-eight members of the faculty wrote an open letter to Dean Smith demanding a better understanding of "the impact online courses will have on the higher-education system as a whole."[15]

Faculty on other campuses were skeptical too. On April 16, the faculty at Amherst College voted down a proposal to join edX, arguing that Amherst was "best served by having the College itself, rather than an outside organization that offers so-called massive open online courses, develop and offer these online courses and course materials."[16] After Amherst announced its decision, the *Chronicle of Higher Education* reported that the faculty at the school were worried about creating "the conditions for the obsolescence of the B.A. degree."[17]

Everywhere that spring, faculty seemed to be waking up to the threat posed by platforms for online learning. On April 26 at Duke, the faculty voted against working with 2U to offer online courses for credit. Doing so, they claimed, would allow their students to "watch recorded lectures and participate in sections via Web cam— enjoying neither the advantages of self-paced learning nor the responsiveness of a professor who teaches to the passions and curiosities of students."[18]

Members of the philosophy department at San Jose State University went one step further, criticizing not just online educational platforms but also the professors who chose to work with them. On April 29, they sent an open letter to Harvard's Michael Sandel, taking him to task for teaching his popular Justice class on edX. "Professors who care about public education," they wrote, "should not produce products that will replace professors, dismantle departments, and provide a diminished education for students in public universities."[19] The letter was signed "In solidarity, the SJSU Philosophy Department."

Faculty also voiced their objections in public policy debates. That summer in California, for example, they worked successfully to persuade the state legislature to shelve a bill that would have allowed students who were unable to register for oversubscribed introductory courses in California's higher education system to receive credit from approved online providers.[20] The bill was introduced in March by state senator Darrell

Steinberg in reaction to a 2012 study that had found that nearly 20 percent of the 2.4 million students in the California community college system were unable to register for a class because it was already full.[21]

Faculty objections to new educational technologies didn't stop in 2013. They've continued to this day. While the University of Pittsburgh's students were praising Pitt's August 2019 partnership with Outlier as a way to deliver quality education "at a lower price than the cost of in-person classes,"[22] the University of Pittsburgh's faculty were looking for ways to scuttle the deal. "It is important," one of them wrote, "that all courses for Pitt credit are designed with input from Pitt faculty."[23] Another argued that Outlier's Introduction to Psychology class shouldn't count for Pitt credit—because "For every other Pitt psychology class, you can directly email your instructor or stop by office hours."[24]

I think you get the idea. Right from the start, every technological innovation that we've discussed in this book has faced fierce resistance from faculty at traditional institutions who might understandably be worried about the threat these innovations pose to their powerful position in the current model of higher education. After all, once you accept that online learning creates benefits for students and those benefits are likely to improve considerably over time—and that the diploma, not the education, is why many students pay us so much money—then you have to accept that online education and online credentialing pose a direct threat to that model.

In that light, it's understandable that many of us in academia might look out for ourselves in how we respond to new technologies that might damage our careers. "A professor must have an incentive to adopt new technology," a colleague recently told me. "I am a tenured old fart and can simply wait out this shock until retirement. Innovation adoption will occur one funeral at a time."

But as we do that, we should also recognize that people outside the academy are paying attention to our behavior. When I spoke with one prominent educational entrepreneur about how strongly most faculty are resisting online learning, he summed up the logic of the resistance this way: "Faculty are telling students, 'If you can't afford the *foie gras* I'm serving, then you deserve to starve.'"

*   *   *

If you've made it this far with me in this book, you know the big-picture argument I've been trying to make: new technologies—and the new forms of learning and credentialing they enable—represent a rare opportunity for us to address the manifest inequities of our current system of higher education and expand it to serve a much greater range of students.

The word *expand* is key. Online education isn't going to replace the four-year residential degree. We'll always have terrific colleges and universities that can provide that kind of education, and as a society, we'll always benefit from what they provide. But for the first time in a long time, we also have the ability to reach hundreds of thousands of students who traditionally haven't had access to those institutions. They're surely as deserving of educational opportunity as anybody else, and we can now give it to them.

Who could be opposed to that?

A lot of people. Most are higher-ed insiders who worry that their way of doing things, and indeed their whole livelihood, is under threat. Above, I cited the example of Cary Nelson, the outgoing president of the American Association of University Professors, who insisted in 2012 that online learning was "not education" and dismissed it as best suited for people in retirement homes ("where folks are unlikely to assume any social responsibilities for the 'knowledge' they have acquired").[25]

That's pretty extreme, but Nelson is far from alone in his outlook. In fact, a whole chorus of higher-ed insiders has been singing this tune for the past decade. Here's a quick sampling:

Mark Edmundson, professor, University of Virginia, 2012: "Online education is a one-size-fits-all endeavor. It tends to be a monologue and not a real dialogue. . . . A real course creates intellectual joy, at least in some. I don't think an Internet course ever will."[26]

Robert Talbert, professor, Grand Valley State University, 2012: "Khan Academy is great for learning about lots of different subjects. But it's not really adequate for learning those subjects on a level that really makes a difference in the world."[27]

Bob Samuels, professor, University of California at Santa Barbara, 2013: "Online education . . . often functions to undermine the values of university professors . . . the role of the teachers is being eliminated."[28]

John Warner, professor, College of Charleston, 2015: "Arizona State looks like a dystopia, rather than a model for the future. ASU is pretty clearly set up as a factory of credentialing, and any lip-service to educational excellence, particularly in the undergraduate sphere, is exactly that."[29]

Joshua Kim, director of online programs and strategy, Dartmouth Center for the Advancement of Learning, 2020: "New types of lower-cost online education may provide many benefits to adult working professionals. But the cost may be to accelerate the financial challenges of already stressed regionally-known and tuition-dependent colleges and universities."[30]

Lisa Wheelahan, professor, University of Toronto, 2022: "Rather than presenting new opportunities for social inclusion and access to education, [credentialing platforms] contribute to the privatisation of education by unbundling the curriculum and blurring the line between public and private provision in higher education."[31]

I could go on.

Do you detect a note of condescension in those various remarks? I do. I'm sure it's not intentional, but it's definitely there—and I can't resist gently pushing back.

Professor Edmundson, I agree with you that joy is an admirable goal for higher education. But what about the many people from all walks and stages of life who are unfairly excluded from our pricey time- and location-bound residential degrees? Should they not also be our concern? Professor Talbert, if students can learn math, science, history, or economics from Khan Academy for free, at the time and place of their choosing, might that not help them make a difference in the world? Professor Samuels, does increasing educational opportunity for those who previously haven't had access to it *really* undermine the values of university professors—and if it does, shouldn't that make us question university professors' values? Professor Warner, Arizona State may not be Harvard or Stanford, but more than fourteen thousand undergraduates enroll there each year, almost half of whom come from minority backgrounds and almost a third of whom are first-generation college students.[32] That should count for something, shouldn't it? Dr. Kim, shouldn't we be excited about new ways of learning that "may provide many benefits to adult working professionals" rather than worried about putting stress on "tuition-dependent colleges and universities"? And Professor Wheelahan, why, exactly, is "unbundling the curriculum" a problem? If online platforms can put individual classes online for anybody to take, doesn't that do something to help us achieve the goals of social inclusion and access to education?

You know my take on what's happening here: I'm concerned the faculty members who are resisting the innovations that we've talked about in this book are focused too much on protecting our *model* of education and not nearly enough on pursuing our *mission* to serve the needs of our students and of society.

Do we really believe that learning can occur only when degree curricula are designed by faculty members employed by the universities offering those degrees? If so, what do we make of Advanced Placement credits and transfer credits? Do we really believe that the measure of a quality education is whether a credentialed faculty member is available to answer student emails and hold office hours? If so, what do we make of a study by Florida Polytechnic University finding that students who took Outlier's calculus class passed at a higher rate than those who took the on-campus class?[33] If prerecorded lectures are inferior to a live performance, what do we make of Professor Khosrow Ghadiri's finding that student success rates in his Electronics and Circuits class at San Jose State went up dramatically after he started using recorded edX lectures from MIT's Anant Agarwal?[34]

I understand why so many of my colleagues feel threatened by the changes we've been discussing. They threaten me too—but not enough to make me feel that it's okay to defend a deeply unjust system in which tuition has increased at four times the rate of inflation for almost a half century; in which graduates have incurred $1.7 trillion in student-loan debt; and in which students born into the top 1 percent of the income distribution are seventy-seven times more likely to gain access to elite education than students from the bottom 20 percent. These are systemic problems, and we're unlikely to solve them from within. Are we really comfortable standing "in solidarity" against new digital technologies and platforms that can help address these problems?

To be fair, this isn't the first time that we in higher education have banded together to resist changes that we feel threaten the world we've devoted our lives to. Nor is it the first time that we've revealed a bias against expanding our reach. In 1944, for example, many people in the academy strongly opposed the GI Bill—because, to put it plainly, they felt it would bring the wrong kind of people into the system.

If you doubt that's true, consider that in 1944, Robert Maynard Hutchins, the president of the University of Chicago, worried that if colleges and universities admitted great numbers of returning soldiers through the GI Bill, those institutions would "find themselves converted into educational hobo jungles."[35] And James B. Conant, the president of Harvard, worried that the GI Bill failed "to distinguish between those who can profit most from advanced education and those who cannot." This made Conant worry that "we may find the least capable among the war generation . . . flooding the facilities for advanced education."[36]

All of this barbarians-at-the-gates talk sounds ridiculous today, and the GI Bill is widely celebrated as a success. After all, it increased access to higher education, boosted individual prosperity, jumpstarted the postwar economy, and transformed the lives of millions of Americans.

Sounds pretty good to me.

IV
Commencement

12

Rediscovering Our Mission: A Summation—and a Path Forward—for Educators

The GI Bill represented a transformative moment in the history of American higher education and American society. But I believe we've now arrived at a moment with even more transformative potential. That's because we at last have the ability to address the three scarcities that for centuries have limited what we can do in higher education—the scarcities of access, instruction, and credentials.

People all over the world are already benefiting from this new abundance of nontraditional educational opportunity, whether those of us in higher education like it or not. And it's worth showcasing just a few of their stories to counterbalance all of the skepticism I quoted in the previous chapter.

David Reed, an aluminum mill worker in West Virginia, pursued an online BS degree in biochemistry through Arizona State University with the goal of preparing himself for medical school—no small feat, given that he was not only working full-time but also raising twin boys. "ASU was the only option that gave me the opportunity to complete the courses I needed, and continue to work and provide for my family," he says. Reed is currently in his second year of medical school at Marshall University in West Virginia.[1]

There's also Battushig Myanganbayar, the fifteen-year-old Mongolian high school student whose experience with edX we discussed in chapter 7. After taking the Circuits and Electronics MOOC taught by MIT's Anant Agarwal, Myanganbayar received a perfect score, was accepted to MIT on the strength of that performance, earned a BS and an MS, and was hired by Apple. Today he works as the CTO of a company that he recently cofounded.[2]

Balesh Jindal, a physician in India, took a Coursera class in social psychology and used what she learned to educate two thousand female students age four to seventeen about the issue of sex abuse.[3] Based on the stories she heard from the students, she expanded her practice to address sexual violence occurring in the rural communities she works with.[4]

Mark Halberstadt was almost left behind by the one-size-fits-all pace of traditional education. In a video posted to YouTube in 2011, he describes himself as someone who just wasn't smart enough to do a math-based degree like electrical engineering. After graduating from the University of Denver in 2007, he discovered Khan Academy—and the ability to learn math at his own pace. "I wouldn't have been able to get the type of help that I got from the Khan Academy really anywhere else," he said in his video.[5] After mastering a lot of math at his own pace on Khan Academy, Halberstadt enrolled in Temple University's electrical engineering program and in 2014 graduated *summa cum laude*. He currently works as a software engineer at Google.[6]

Chelsea Rucker, a single mother, discovered Google's self-directed IT certification program after moving out of a homeless shelter in Nashville. While working full-time at Goodwill, Rucker completed the course and landed a position at Google as a data center technician. "Nobody ever talks about how this is possible," she says. "If we become well-versed in technology, we'll find all kinds of opportunities."[7]

Could any of these people have succeeded in the way they did without the opportunity to pursue online learning? Is it really true that they haven't assumed "any social responsibilities for the 'knowledge' they have acquired"? Was their educational experience really dystopic? Of course not.

I know that not everybody who takes advantage of these new kinds of learning and credentialing will be as successful as the people I've just described, and not all of them will be able to rub elbows with the world's greatest professors. It's even possible that the majority of those who enroll for online courses and certificates and degrees won't finish. But is that really a fatal flaw, given the absolute numbers?

I don't think so. In 2021, Coursera reported that it served 92 million registered learners during the year, including 3.8 million students on 3,600 college campuses.[8] That same year, edX reported having had 110 million enrollments since its founding and said it was currently serving 130,000 students at 465 institutions in 72 countries around the world.[9] Even if only 5 percent of those people finish what they start, that's still a lot of people. You could do a similar calculation with SNHU and ASU, two of the nontraditional universities discussed in this book. Collectively, some 189,000 online students are enrolled at those two institutions,[10] and 29,000 of them receive degrees each year.[11] That, too, is a lot of people—and we haven't covered all of the bases. In 2019, according to the National Center for Education Statistics, 37 percent (7.3 million) of all US higher-education students took at least one online class, and 17.5 percent (3.4 million) students were enrolled in exclusively online programs.[12] The NCES gathered those numbers before the pandemic. They're surely higher today.

From an economic perspective, this all amounts to a significant increase in supply—which is an excellent thing because, according to reports about the great resignation, there is a lot of unmet demand in the workplace.

Promisingly, employers are recognizing that if they relax their degree requirements and instead focus on skills rather than degrees in their hiring, they suddenly have access to a much larger and more diverse pool of potential employees, especially now that so many

people have access to nontraditional forms of education, training, and certification. A 2022 report from
Burning Glass Institute projects that "1.4 million jobs
could open to workers without college degrees over the
next five years."[13] And it's not just workers who could
benefit. So could the demographic that Will Bunch, in
*After the Ivory Tower Falls: How College Broke the Ameri-
can Dream and Blew Up Our Politics*, describes as the "Left
Out"—that is, the "4.6 million Americans between the
age of eighteen and twenty-four who aren't attending
school or working a full-time job."[14]

*   *   *

You may have noticed while reading the previous chapter that the objections being raised by higher education
insiders today sound a lot like the objections raised by
entertainment industry executives in the mid-2010s.
What's important to realize is eventually those executives *did* accept the changes that new technologies
were making possible, and as a result, the industry is
thriving, financially and creatively. Imagine that! If a
decade ago you'd told entertainment industry insiders that Amazon, Apple, and Netflix would win Oscars
and Emmys and produce a mind-boggling quantity of
high-quality movies and TV and that the major studios
would choose to chase that success by throwing themselves wholeheartedly behind Disney Plus, HBO Max,
Hulu, and Peacock, they would have cocked their heads,
given you a very odd look, and laughed you out of the

room. But because the industry has embraced change instead of resisting it, we're now living in a new golden age of entertainment.

So what happened? How did entertainment executives move past their resistance to change?

They did it by worrying less about their old model for doing business and instead focusing on doing whatever they could to advance their mission—which, they realized, wasn't selling more shiny plastic disks at $20 a pop or more tickets on opening weekend in the nation's movie theaters. Their mission was to create great entertainment and get it in front of the right audience. If pursuing that mission meant doing things differently, then so be it.

The entertainment industry is very different from the education industry. But in both cases, defining the mission is critical to finding the courage to embrace change. And that raises the critical question: what *is* the mission of higher education?

I'm honestly not sure we know.

I say that because I recently took a look at the mission statements of the top ten universities in the *US News & World Report* rankings and found them to contain very little of the clarity and specificity that define strong mission statements—which is to say, mission statements that can inspire and guide action. I'm sorry to say that my own university, Carnegie Mellon, has a mission statement that's typical of the genre. Here's how it reads, in full:

To create a transformative educational experience
for students focused on deep disciplinary knowledge;
problem solving; leadership, communication,
and interpersonal skills; and personal health and
well-being.

To cultivate a transformative university community
committed to (a) attracting and retaining diverse,
world-class talent; (b) creating a collaborative
environment open to the free exchange of ideas, where
research, creativity, innovation, and entrepreneurship
can flourish; and (c) ensuring individuals can achieve
their full potential.

To impact society in a transformative way—
regionally, nationally, and globally—by engaging
with partners outside the traditional borders of the
university campus.[15]

What does that all mean? I've read it many times, and I still have no idea. I imagine a good number of my colleagues at Carnegie Mellon would have a similar reaction—which means that this statement isn't doing what it's supposed to, which is to help us focus on a common goal.[16]

So what *is* our mission, and how can we define it more clearly and concisely?

I'm biased, but I like the idea that I propose in chapter 1: *Our mission is to create opportunities for as many students as possible to discover and develop their unique talents so they can use those talents to make a difference in the world.* I think that's a pretty straightforward statement of why we're here and what we should aspire to do—and nothing in that statement requires us to stick with our increasingly obsolete and unjust factory model of delivering education to students disproportionately drawn from wealth and privilege.

If we think more clearly about our mission, we can think more creatively about how to achieve it. Consider the sage-on-a-stage model of teaching. When information was hard to transmit, it made sense for every college and university to employ professors teaching all of the standard disciplines. But that's no longer true today. As François Ortalo-Magné asked in 2014 when he was the dean of the University of Wisconsin's business school: how many calculus professors do we *really* need in a world of online instruction? "Maybe it's nine," he wrote. "My colleague says it's four. One to teach in English, one in French, one in Chinese, and one in the farm system in case one dies."[17] Whatever the number, it's a lot fewer than what we have today.

Thinking in that way is scary for me (how many people do we really need to teach what *I* teach?), but I genuinely believe that embracing technological change is the only way for us to start creating an affordable system of higher education that's accessible to anybody who wants it.

A newly clear sense of mission will also help us reimagine much of what we do. Is it really still true that for all students the best education is delivered by somebody with a doctoral degree and a long list of academic publications? Is it really still true that for all students the best teaching and learning happens in-person in a classroom for a few hours a week during a fourteen-week semester? Those ideas made sense for a long time, but do they make sense today, given how many other options are possible and given everything that we're learning about how differently people learn? Surely not.

Now that lifelong learning is a possibility, we might also want to reimagine the whole bundle of knowledge—that is, the curriculum—that we offer undergraduates before sending them off into the world. When access to instruction was scarce, colleges and universities had to focus on delivering just-in-case knowledge, as in, "You might need to know this someday, and it would be hard to pick it up later, so we're going to teach it to you now. Just in case." But with access to instruction becoming abundant, we might want to shift to a just-in-time model of education, at least in some fields, as in, "We'll teach you what you need to know right now, and if you find you need something else, feel free to come back later." This model might be particularly well suited to technology fields, where so much is changing so fast that much of what students learn today is likely to be irrelevant five years from now.

As academics, we're extremely well positioned to make these kinds of transitions, and in my view, we have a moral imperative to do so. These days, we spend a lot of time teaching our students to recognize and relinquish their privileged position in society so that underprivileged members of society can flourish. Shouldn't we ask the same of ourselves?

There's also a practical reason for us to move from protecting our business model to advancing our mission: we don't have a choice. A financially unsustainable system can last for only so long before taxpayers decide to stop bailing it out.[18] A morally unsustainable system can last for only so long before those who are left behind start to demand justice. For a long time, society was willing to look past the financial expense and moral injustice of higher education because it didn't have any other good options for creating educated adults. Today's online learning platforms change that dynamic in ways that I think we in higher education need to take seriously. We have a once-in-a-lifetime opportunity today to create a more open, flexible, inclusive, and lower-priced system of higher education that can scale to accommodate the hundreds of thousands of capable students who today are left behind. If we embrace that opportunity, think about how much value we might create for those students, and how much value those students might create for society.

If we want to help as many students as possible develop their unique talents and use them to make a difference in the world, then it's time to start asking urgent questions about how we can actually *do* that. Can we deliver a high-quality education to whole populations that have long been excluded from our current system of education? Can we find new kinds of educators out there who are willing and able to deliver their knowledge to students? Can we use new information-rich digital platforms to customize the education we provide to students in ways that no classroom-bound model can match? Can we create new ways for nontraditional learners to communicate their skills and knowledge to employers? Can we become active and vibrant participants in an educational transformation that will address the many socioeconomic injustices of our current system? I strongly believe that the answer to all of these questions is the same: yes, we can.

So let's get going. It's time to move beyond our narrow self-interest, embrace the changes that are coming, and start creating a new golden age of education—for our students, for society, and for ourselves.

Acknowledgments

Writing this book has been far more challenging, and far more rewarding, than I imagined—and I want to pause and thank the many people who provided the support, guidance, wisdom, and encouragement that made this book possible.

To Kristen Yeager, thank you for sharing your incredible research skills, your excellent understanding of the education literature, and your amazing patience. Time and again I came to you with impossible research questions, and each time you returned with exactly the information and knowledge I needed to push this book forward.

To Toby Lester, thanks for partnering with me in writing another book—particularly after all I put you through on the first book. You have the uncanny skill and ability to take my random thoughts and ideas and to turn them into exactly what I knew I wanted to say. Without your help, advice, and patience, I'm quite sure I'd still be rewriting chapter 1.

I am indebted to my colleagues at the Heinz College at Carnegie Mellon University for allowing me to be part of a great community of scholars. In particular, I'd like to thank Rahul Telang for partnering on the industry research that led to this book, and for Pedro Ferreira for partnering on the education research that I hope will follow this book. I'd also like to thank Dean Ramayya Krishnan for supporting our vision of creating the Initiative for Teaching and Education Analytics to study ways to create a more fair, equitable, and abundant system of education.

I'm incredibly thankful to Erik Brynjolfsson for being my advisor, coach, and mentor at MIT. I couldn't have asked for a better example of what it means to be a scholar.

I thank Susan Buckley, Deborah Cantor-Adams, and the team at the MIT Press for taking a chance on a book that goes against the grain of the conventional wisdom in the academy.

None of this would have been possible without the love and support of my dear wife, Rhonda. Thank you for believing in me when I haven't believed in myself, and for encouraging me to try so many things I didn't think I could do. I also want to thank our kids, Davis, Cole, and Molly, for the joy you've brought into our lives—and particularly my son, Cole, whose tireless pursuit of justice inspired me to write this book.

Finally, I thank Jesus Christ, the ultimate provider of justice in a world of injustice and abundance in a world of scarcity.

Notes

Preface

1. Lawrence Biemiller, "In Her Own Words, Joyce Carol Oates Is a Teacher First," *Chronicle of Higher Education*, November 17, 2014, https://www.chronicle.com/article/in-her-own-words-joyce-carol -oates-is-a-teacher-first.

2. Elaine Showalter, "Joyce Carol Oates Honored at Retirement Gala," *Washington Post*, November 9, 2014, https://www.washing tonpost.com/news/arts-and-entertainment/wp/2014/11/09/joyce -carol-oates-honored-at-retirement-gala.

3. Albert Jiang, "Princeton Admits Record-Low 3.98% of Applicants in Historic Application Cycle," *Daily Princetonian*, April 6, 2021, https://www.dailyprincetonian.com/article/2021/04/princeton-college -admissions-class-of-2025-ivy-league.

4. Dana Goldstein and Jack Healy, "Inside the Pricey, Totally Legal World of College Consultants," *New York Times*, March 13, 2019, https://www.nytimes.com/2019/03/13/us/admissions-cheating-scandal -consultants.html.

5. "Fees & Payment Options," Undergraduate Admission, Princeton University, accessed September 21, 2022, https://admission.princeton .edu/cost-aid/fees-payment-options.

6. Princeton is arguably the most generous of the Ivy League colleges when it comes to financial aid. In September 2022, Princeton

announced that it was making tuition and room and board free for all students from families making less than $100,000 per year (an increase from the previous $65,000 annual income threshold for free tuition). Princeton's website said the free tuition is likely to apply to 25 percent of the school's undergraduate students. Emily Aronson, "Princeton Will Enhance Its Groundbreaking Financial Aid Program," Office of Communication, Princeton University, September 8, 2022, https://www.princeton.edu/news/2022/09/08/princeton-will -enhance-its-groundbreaking-financial-aid-program.

7. Jennifer Altmann, "Acclaimed Author Oates to Retire from University," *Princeton Alumni Weekly*, March 6, 2013, https://paw.princeton .edu/article/acclaimed-author-oates-retire-university.

8. Clark Kerr, *The Uses of the University*, 5th ed. (Cambridge, MA: Harvard University Press, 2001).

9. Abigail Johnson Hess, "U.S. Student Debt Has Increased by More than 100% over the Past 10 Years," *CNBC*, December 22, 2020, https://www.cnbc.com/2020/12/22/us-student-debt-has-increased-by -more-than-100percent-over-past-10-years.html.

10. Brandon Busteed, "Higher Education's Work Preparation Paradox," *Gallup*, February 25, 2014, https://news.gallup.com/opinion /gallup/173249/higher-education-work-preparation-paradox.aspx.

11. Meg James, "Fox's Chase Carey Calls a la Carte Programming 'a Fantasy,'" *Los Angeles Times*, August 8, 2013, https://www.latimes .com/entertainment/envelope/cotown/la-et-ct-foxs-chase-carey-calls -ala-carte-a-fantasy-20130808-story.html.

12. Mi Zhou, George H. Chen, Pedro Ferreira, and Michael D. Smith, "Consumer Behavior in the Online Classroom: Using Video Analytics and Machine Learning to Understand the Consumption of Video Courseware," *Journal of Marketing Research* 58, no. 6 (2021): 1079–1100.

Chapter 1

1. President's Commission on Higher Education, *Higher Education for American Democracy: A Report of the President's Commission on Higher*

Education, Vol. 1, *Establishing the Goals* (New York: Harper & Brothers, 1947), 23.

2. Raj Chetty, John N. Friedman, Emmanuel Saez, Nicholas Turner, and Danny Yagan, "Mobility Report Cards: The Role of Colleges in Intergenerational Mobility," National Bureau of Economic Research Working Paper 23618, July 2017.

3. Gregor Aisch, Larry Buchanan, Amanda Cox, and Kevin Quealy, "Some Colleges Have More Students from the Top 1 Percent than the Bottom 60. Find Yours," *New York Times*, January 18, 2017, https:// www.nytimes.com/interactive/2017/01/18/upshot/some-colleges-have -more-students-from-the-top-1-percent-than-the-bottom-60.html.

4. See Chetty et al., "Mobility Report Cards."

5. Horace Mann, *Life and Works of Horace Mann* (Boston: Lee and Shepard, 1891), 251.

6. Scott Carlson, "Why the College Degree Is a Signal—and Why That Should Worry You," *Chronicle of Higher Education*, March 19, 2019, https://www.chronicle.com/newsletter/the-edge/2019-03-19.

7. Pell Institute for the Study of Opportunity in Higher Education and Penn Ahead Alliance for Higher Education and Democracy, "Indicators of Higher Education Equity in the United States: 2018 Historical Trend Report," accessed August 30, 2022, http://pellinsti tute.org/downloads/publications-Indicators_of_Higher_Education _Equity_in_the_US_2018_Historical_Trend_Report.pdf.

8. See, for example, Dominic Brewer, Eric R. Eide, and Ronald G. Ehrenberg, "Does It Pay to Attend an Elite Private College? Cross-Cohort Evidence on the Effects of College Type on Earnings," *Journal of Human Resources* 34, no. 1 (1999): 104–123, which finds that, after controlling for other confounding variables, attending a "top" university was causally associated with a 20 percent wage premium in 1980 versus only a 9 percent wage premium in 1972. Similarly, Mark Hoekstra, "The Effect of Attending the Flagship State University on Earnings: A Discontinuity-Based Approach," *Review of Economics and Statistics* 91, no. 4 (2009): 717–724, shows that students who were "barely" admitted to a flagship state university had a 20 percent wage

premium after graduation over similar students who were "barely" rejected by the same flagship university.

9. See, for example, Vasyl Taras, Grishma Shah, Marjaana Gunkel, and Ernesto Tavoletti, "Graduates of Elite Universities Get Paid More. Do They Perform Better?," *Harvard Business Review*, September 4, 2020, https://hbr.org/2020/09/graduates-of-elite-universities-get-paid -more-do-they-perform-better, which cites the results from an academic study by Vasyl Taras, Marjaana Gunkel, Alexander Assouad, Ernesto Tavoletti, Justin Kraemer, Alfredo Jiménez, Anna Svirina, Weng Si Lei, and Grishma Shah, "The Predictive Power of University Pedigree on the Graduate's Performance in Global Virtual Teams," *European Journal of International Management* 16, no. 4 (2021): 555–584.

10. See Chetty et al., "Mobility Report Cards," where the authors define Ivy-plus colleges as "the eight Ivy League colleges, University of Chicago, Stanford, MIT, and Duke," and "elite" schools as the eighty most selective universities in the United States as ranked by *Barron's*.

11. Jenny Anderson, "America's Top Colleges Are Not the Engines of Social Mobility They Say They Are," Quartz, September 13, 2019, https://qz.com/1706334/college-admissions-are-a-game-that-still -favors-rich-over-poor.

12. President's Commission on Higher Education, *Higher Education for American Democracy*, Vol. 1, *Establishing the Goal*, 67.

13. Michael Provasnik and Michael Planty, *Community Colleges: Special Supplement to The Condition of Education 2008* (NCES 2008-033) (Washington, DC: National Center for Education Statistics, Institute of Education Sciences, US Department of Education, August 2008), iii, 2.

14. Richard V. Reeves, "College and the End of Upward Mobility," *Chronicle of Higher Education*, December 3, 2017, https://www.chron icle.com/article/college-and-the-end-of-upward-mobility; with similar quotes in Anthony P. Carnevale, Peter Schmidt, and Jeff Strohl, "How Higher Ed Can Stop Affirmative Action for Rich White People," *Chronicle of Higher Education*, July 8, 2020, https://www.chronicle .com/article/how-higher-ed-can-stop-affirmative-action-for-rich

-white-people ("Higher education is the capstone of an educational system that sorts winners from losers and always invests in the winners. It magnifies the inequality dutifully delivered to it by the public school system and projects it further into labor markets where it creates new waves of advantages that guarantee the intergenerational reproduction of class and racial privilege"); and Karin Fischer, "The Barriers to Mobility: Why Higher Ed's Promise Remains Unfulfilled," *Chronicle of Higher Education*, December 30, 2019, https://www.chron icle.com/article/why-higher-ed-rsquo-s-promise-remains-unfulfilled ("The better off you are, the more likely you are to go to college. If you go to college, you are likely to be better off").

15. Chetty et al., "Mobility Report Cards."

16. Josh Mitchell, "The Long Road to the Student Debt Crisis," *Wall Street Journal*, June 7, 2019, https://www.wsj.com/articles/the-long -road-to-the-student-debt-crisis-11559923730.

17. Jennifer Glynn, "Opening Doors: How Selective Colleges and Universities Are Expanding Access for High-Achieving, Low-Income Students," Jack Kent Cooke Foundation, accessed August 31, 2022, https://www.jkcf.org/research/opening-doors-how-selective-colleges -and-universities-are-expanding-access-for-high-achieving-low -income-students.

18. "As part of the American Recovery and Reinvestment Act of 2009, the maximum Pell award amount increased from \$4,730 to \$5,350 and the federal government also increased Pell funding. Total federal expenditure on Pell increased from \$19.8 billion in 2008–09 to \$33.2 billion in 2009–10 to \$39.0 billion in 2010–11 but fell to \$35.4 billion in 2011–12 and to \$33.3 billion in 2012–13." See also Jennifer Giancola and Richard D. Kahlenberg, "True Merit: Ensuring Our Brightest Students Have Access to Our Best Colleges and Universities," Jack Kent Cooke Foundation, accessed August 31, 2022, https://www.jkcf.org/research/true-merit-ensuring-our-brightest -students-have-access-to-our-best-colleges-and-universities.

19. David Plunkert, "The Long Road to the Student Debt Crisis," *Wall Street Journal*, June 8, 2019, https://www.wsj.com/articles/the -long-road-to-the-student-debt-crisis-11559923730.

20. Institution for Higher Education Policy, "Cost," IHEP Postsecondary Data GPS, accessed August 31, 2022, https://datagps.ihep.org/chapters/chapter-4.

21. Caroline Hoxby, "College Choices Have Consequences," Stanford Institute for Economic Policy Research (SIEPR), December 2012, https://siepr.stanford.edu/research/publications/college-choices-have-consequences.

22. Hoxby, "College Choices Have Consequences."

23. Tyler Ransom, "SFFAvHarvard-Docs / TrialExhibits / P104.pdf," GitHub, September 18, 2019, https://github.com/tyleransom/SFFAvHarvard-Docs/blob/master/TrialExhibits/P104.pdf.

24. Ransom, "SFFAvHarvard-Docs / TrialExhibits / P106.pdf."

25. T. Rees Shapiro, "At U-VA., a 'Watch List' Flags VIP Applicants for Special Handling," *Washington Post*, April 1, 2017, https://www.washingtonpost.com/local/education/at-u-va-a-watch-list-flags-vip-applicants-for-special-handling/2017/04/01/9482b256-106e-11e7-9d5a-a83e627dc120_story.html. A 2019 article in the *Wall Street Journal* drew a similar conclusion that the University of Southern California "explicitly weighed how much money applicants' families could donate when determining whether to admit students," after the *Journal* reviewed USC's list of "VIP" applicants—a list that contained notations like "given 2 million already," "1 mil pledge," "previously donated $25k to Heritage Hall," and "father is surgeon"; see Jennifer Levitz and Melissa Korn, "'Father Is Surgeon,' '1 Mil Pledge': The Role of Money in USC Admissions," *Wall Street Journal*, September 3, 2019, https://www.wsj.com/articles/father-is-surgeon-1-mil-pledge-the-role-of-money-in-usc-admissions-11567548124.

26. Jamie Myers and Zachary Zettler, "Repurposeability: The Future of College Campuses," *Building Design + Construction*, October 14, 2020, https://www.bdcnetwork.com/repurposeability-future-college-campuses.

27. Nikil Saval, "If You Build It, They Will Come . . . Won't They?," *New York Times*, September 10, 2015, https://www.nytimes.com/2015/09/13/magazine/if-you-build-it-they-will-come-wont-they.html.

28. Jon Marcus, "The Hidden Reason College Costs Keep Climbing," *The Atlantic*, July 25, 2016, https://www.theatlantic.com/education /archive/2016/07/the-paradox-of-new-buildings-on-campus/492398.

29. William Baumol, David de Ferranti, Monte Malach, Ariel Pablos-Méndez, Hilary Tabish, and Lilian Gomory Wu, *The Cost Disease: Why Computers Get Cheaper and Health Care Doesn't* (New Haven, CT: Yale University Press, 2013).

30. William J. Baumol and William G. Bowen, *Performing Arts: The Economic Dilemma* (New York: Twentieth Century Fund, 1966).

31. William J. Baumol, "Macroeconomics of Unbalanced Growth: The Anatomy of Urban Crisis," *American Economic Review* 57, no. 3 (1967): 415–426.

32. Douglas Belkin, "For Sale: SAT-Takers' Names. Colleges Buy Student Data and Boost Exclusivity," *Wall Street Journal*, November 7, 2019, https://www.wsj.com/articles/for-sale-sat-takers-names-colleges -buy-student-data-and-boost-exclusivity-11572976621.

33. See, for example, Paul Tough, *The Years That Matter Most: How College Makes or Breaks US* (Boston: Houghton Mifflin Harcourt, 2019), particularly chapter 3, "Fixing the Test"; and Ann Carrns, "Another College Expense: Preparing for the SAT and Act," *New York Times*, October 29, 2014, https://www.nytimes.com/2014/10/29/your -money/another-college-expense-preparing-for-the-sat-and-act-.html.

34. David Radwin, Johnathan G. Conzelmann, Annaliza Nunnery, T. Austin Lacy, Joanna Wu, Stephen Lew, Jennifer Wine, Peter Siegel, and Tracy Hunt-White, *2015–16 National Postsecondary Student Aid Survey (NSASP:16): Student Financial Aid Estimates for 2015–16. First Look* (NCES 2018-466) (Washington, DC: National Center for Education Statistics, Institute for Education Sciences, US Department of Education, January 2018), https://nces.ed.gov/pubs2018/2018466 .pdf, table 4, p. 13. Aid is defined as "all institutional need- and merit-based grants, scholarships, tuition waivers, loans, and work-study assistance funded by the institution attended."

35. See Daniel Golden, "How a Rotten System Enabled Rick Singer's Fraud," *Chronicle of Higher Education*, September 22, 2021, https://

www.chronicle.com/article/how-a-rotten-system-enabled-rick-singers
-fraud; and New York City Department of Education, "Report on
Guidance Counselors," accessed August 31, 2022, https://infohub
.nyced.org/docs/default-source/default-document-library/guidance
-counselor-report-and-summary-feb-2019.pdf.

Chapter 2

1. *The Harvard University Catalogue, 1874–75* (Cambridge, MA:
Charles W. Sever, 1874), 24, 61.

2. Ronald Story, "Harvard Students, the Boston Elite, and the New
England Preparatory System, 1800–1876," *History of Education Quarterly* 15, no. 3 (1975): 281–298.

3. Thomas D. Snyder, ed., *120 Years of American Education: A Statistical Portrait* (Washington, DC: National Center for Education
Statistics, Office of Educational Research and Development, US
Department of Education, January 1993), https://nces.ed.gov/pubs93
/93442.pdf.

4. Cornell Law School Legal Information Institute, "7 U.S. Code §
304—Investment of Proceeds of Sale of Land or Scrip," *Cornell Law
School Legal Information Institute*, accessed August 31, 2022, https://
www.law.cornell.edu/uscode/text/7/304.

5. David B. Hawk, "Specialization in American Higher Education and
the 'General Education' Movement," *Journal of Educational Sociology*
28, no. 1 (1954): 19–24.

6. John Tagg, *The Instruction Myth: Why Higher Education Is Hard to
Change, and How to Change It* (New Brunswick, NJ: Rutgers University
Press, 2019).

7. Ellwood Patterson Cubberley, *Public School Administration: A Statement of the Fundamental Principles Underlying the Organization and
Administration of Public Education* (Boston: Houghton Mifflin Company, 1916), 335–338, https://www.google.com/books/edition/Public
_School_Administration/Jw8CAAAAYAAJ?hl=en&gbpv=1&pg
=PA335.

8. Immanuel Kant, *The Conflict of the Faculties*, trans. Mary J. Gregor (Lincoln: University of Nebraska Press, 1992), 23.

9. Ellwood Patterson Cubberley, *Public Education in the United States: A Study and Interpretation of American Educational History* (Boston: Houghton Mifflin, 1919), Internet Archive, https://archive.org/details /publiceducationi00cubbuoft.

10. Cubberley, *Public School Administration*.

11. Cubberley, *Public School Administration*.

12. All quotes below from Morris Llewellyn Cooke, *Academic and Industrial Efficiency: A Report to the Carnegie Foundation for the Advancement of Teaching* (New York: Carnegie Foundation for the Advancement of Teaching, 1910), https://www.google.com/books/edition /Academic_and_Industrial_Efficiency/HvkoAAAAYAAJ.

13. "The History of College Rankings," *College Rank*, June 20, 2022, https://www.collegerank.net/history-of-college-rankings.

14. The years 1870 through 1991 come from Snyder, *120 Years of American Education: A Statistical Portrait*, table 24. The years 1992 through 2020 come from National Center for Education Statistics, "Table 101.10. Estimate of Resident Population, by Age Group: 1970 through 2019," Digest of Education Statistics, accessed August 31, 2022, https://nces.ed.gov/programs/digest/d19/tables/dt19_101.10.asp; and from National Center for Education Statistics, "Table 302.60. Percentage of 18- to 24-Year-Olds Enrolled in College, by Level of Institution and Sex and Race/Ethnicity of Student: 1970 through 2018," Digest of Education Statistics, accessed August 31, 2022, https://nces .ed.gov/programs/digest/d19/tables/dt19_302.60.asp. Note that NCES data are reported as a percentage of college-aged students to provide a common reference point over time. As such, the figures mean that the total enrollment in college in 2020 represents 65 percent of the total number of eighteen to twenty-four-year-olds, not that 65 percent of eighteen- to twenty-four-year-olds were enrolled in college in 2020.

15. John R. Thelin, *Essential Documents in the History of American Higher Education* (Baltimore: Johns Hopkins University Press, 2014), 250.

16. "College Board—Form 990 for Period Ending Dec 2018," *Pro-Publica*, May 9, 2013, https://projects.propublica.org/nonprofits/display _990/131623965/01_2020_prefixes_06-13%2F131623965_201812_990 _2020012717070895.

17. College Board, "Over 2.2 Million Students in Class of 2019 Took SAT, Largest Group Ever," *Newsroom*, September 24, 2019, https:// newsroom.collegeboard.org/over-22-million-students-class-2019 -took-sat-largest-group-ever.

18. "Form 990 for Period Ending August 2018," *ProPublica*, May 9, 2013, https://projects.propublica.org/nonprofits/display_990/420841 485/10_2019_prefixes_41-45%2F420841485_201808_990_2019100 416720766.

19. "About ACT," ACT, accessed September 1, 2022, https://www.act. org/content/act/en/about-act.html.

20. James Wellemeyer, "Wealthy Parents Spend up to $10,000 on SAT Prep for Their Kids," *MarketWatch*, July 7, 2019, https://www .marketwatch.com/story/some-wealthy-parents-are-dropping-up-to -10000-on-sat-test-prep-for-their-kids-2019-06-21; "Tutoring & Test Preparation Franchises in the US—Market Size 2005–2028," *IBIS-World*, February 28, 2022, https://www.ibisworld.com/industry-statis tics/market-size/tutoring-test-preparation-franchises-united-states.

21. Robert Morse and Eric Brooks, "How U.S. News Calculated the 2022 Best Colleges Rankings," *U.S. News & World Report*, September 12, 2021, https://www.usnews.com/education/best-colleges/articles /how-us-news-calculated-the-rankings.

22. Robert Morse, "The Birth of the College Rankings," *U.S. News & World Report*, May 16, 2008, https://www.usnews.com/education/best -colleges/articles/how-us-news-calculated-the-rankings.

23. Andrew Gumbel, *Won't Lose This Dream: How an Upstart Urban University Rewrote the Rules of a Broken System* (New York: New Press, 2020), 54. See also William G. Bowen, Matthew M. Chingos, and Michael McPherson, *Crossing the Finish Line: Completing College at America's Public Universities* (Princeton, NJ: Princeton University Press, 2009), 122, which finds that "high school GPA is very positively

and very consistently associated with six-year graduation rates *whatever the level of the high school that the student attended*" (emphasis in original).

24. "2015 Status Report: Georgia State University, Complete College Georgia," Georgia State University, 2015, https://enrollment.gsu.edu/files/2015/08/Georgia-State-University-CCG-Report-2015.pdf; and Benjamin Wermund, "How U.S. News College Rankings Promote Economic Inequality on Campus," *Politico*, September 10, 2017, https://www.politico.com/interactives/2017/top-college-rankings-list-2017-us-news-investigation.

25. Wermund, "How U.S. News College Rankings Promote Economic Inequality on Campus."

26. Wermund, "How U.S. News College Rankings Promote Economic Inequality on Campus."

27. For example, *U.S. News & World Report* dropped Hampshire College from its list of liberal arts institutions after the college decided to go "test-blind" in 2014. See Eric Hoover, "Hampshire College Will Go 'Test Blind,'" *Chronicle of Higher Education*, June 18, 2014, https://www.chronicle.com/blogs/headcount/hampshire-college-will-go-test-blind. Likewise, Trinity College saw its *U.S. News* ranking drop significantly after deemphasizing SAT scores in admissions. Paul Tough, *The Inequality Machine: How College Divides Us* (Boston: Mariner Books, Houghton Mifflin Harcourt, 2021), 187. It also faced pressure to reverse the move in spite of the fact that Trinity's faculty found that the newly admitted class displayed an "intellectual curiosity, openness of mind and spirit, and genuine will to engage with their peers" that exceeded prior classes.

28. Caroline Hoxby, "College Choices Have Consequences," Stanford Institute for Economic Policy Research (SIEPR), December 2012, https://siepr.stanford.edu/research/publications/college-choices-have-consequences.

29. Wermund, "How U.S. News College Rankings Promote Economic Inequality on Campus." See also Shari L. Gnolek, Vincenzo T. Falciano, and Ralph W. Kuncl, "Modeling Change and Variation in U.S.

News & World Report College Rankings: What Would It Really Take to Be in the Top 20?," *Research in Higher Education* 55, no. 8 (2014): 761–779, which shows that a university ranked in the mid-thirties of the *U.S. News* rankings would need to increase spending by $112 million per year to move into the top twenty.

30. David Radwin, Johnathan G. Conzelmann, Annaliza Nunnery, T. Austin Lacy, Joanna Wu, Stephen Lew, Jennifer Wine, Peter Siegel, and Tracy Hunt-White, *2015–16 National Postsecondary Student Aid Survey (NSASP:16): Student Financial Aid Estimates for 2015–16. First Look* (NCES 2018-466) (Washington, DC: National Center for Education Statistics, Institute for Education Sciences, U.S. Department of Education, January 2018), table 4, accessed September 1, 2022, https://nces.ed.gov/pubs2018/2018466.pdf. Aid is defined as "all institutional need- and merit-based grants, scholarships, tuition waivers, loans, and work-study assistance funded by the institution attended."

31. Paul Tough, "What College Admissions Offices Really Want," *New York Times*, September 10, 2019, https://www.nytimes.com/interactive /2019/09/10/magazine/college-admissions-paul-tough.html.

Chapter 3

1. "College Cheating Ringleader Says He Helped More than 750 Families with Admissions Scheme," NBCNews.com, March 13, 2019, https://www.nbcnews.com/news/us-news/college-cheating-master mind-says-he-helped-nearly-800-families-admissions-n982666.

2. Laura Smith, "Affidavit in Support of Criminal Complaint," March 11, 2019, https://www.justice.gov/file/1142876/download.

3. "National Study Shows Dramatic Increase in Hiring Private College Counselors," Independent Education Consultants Association, accessed September 5, 2022, https://www.iecaonline.com/quick-links /ieca-news-center/press/background-information-on-ieca/national -study-shows-dramatic-increase-in-hiring-private-college-counselors.

4. "An Elite Consultant's Take on the College Admissions Scandal," *Wall Street Journal*, March 18, 2019, https://www.wsj.com/video/an

-elite-consultants-take-on-the-college-admissions-scandal/9C7F817E
-FC6A-4A19-A4D2-792856AD18C9.html.

5. "Education Consultants Industry in the US—Market Research
Report," *IBISWorld*, August 28, 2021, https://www.ibisworld.com
/united-states/market-research-reports/education-consultants-industry.

6. "Top 100—Lowest Acceptance Rates," *U.S. News & World Report*,
accessed September 5, 2022, https://www.usnews.com/best-colleges
/rankings/lowest-acceptance-rate.

7. Thomas R. Dye, *Who's Running America? The Obama Reign*, 8th ed.
(London: Routledge, 2017), 203

8. Mark Hoekstra, "The Effect of Attending the Flagship State University on Earnings: A Discontinuity-Based Approach," *Review of Economics and Statistics* 91, no. 4 (2009): 717–724.

9. Douglas Belkin, "For Sale: SAT-Takers' Names. Colleges Buy Student Data and Boost Exclusivity," *Wall Street Journal*, November 7,
2019, https://www.wsj.com/articles/for-sale-sat-takers-names-colleges
-buy-student-data-and-boost-exclusivity-11572976621.

10. Matt Reed, "Admission Follies, with the Girl," Inside Higher Ed,
April 9, 2021, https://www.insidehighered.com/blogs/confessions
-community-college-dean/admission-follies-girl.

11. Willard Dix, "Don't Use College Selectivity as a Measure of Quality," *Forbes*, May 13, 2016, https://www.forbes.com/sites/willarddix
/2016/05/13/dont-use-college-selectivity-as-a-measure-of-quality/?sh
=403ced91821e.

12. Justin Smith, "Acceptance Rate Drops to Record Low 5.9 Percent
for Class of 2023," *Chicago Maroon*, April 1, 2019, https://chicagoma
roon.com/26775/news/uchicago-acceptance-rate-drops-record-low.

13. "Does University of Chicago's Slip in College Ranking Matter?,"
Chicago Magazine, October 23, 2013, https://www.chicagomag.com
/Chicago-Magazine/November-2013/Does-University-of-Chicagos
-Slip-in-College-Ranking-Matter.

14. Deepti Sailappan, "UChicago's U.S. News Ranking Slips to No.
6, after Three Years at No. 3," *Chicago Maroon*, September 9, 2019,

https://chicagomaroon.com/27113/news/uchicago-u-news-ranking-slips-6-three-years-3.

15. Peter Arcidiacono, Josh Kinsler, and Tyler Ransom, "Recruit to Reject? Harvard and African American Applicants," National Bureau of Economic Research Working Paper 26456, November 2019.

16. Steven Johnson, "'Better, Not Bigger': As Private Colleges Hunger for Students, One University Slims Down," *Chronicle of Higher Education*, July 23, 2020, https://www.chronicle.com/article/better-not-bigger-as-private-colleges-hunger-for-students-one-university-slims-down.

17. Nick Anderson, "GWU Aims to Get Smaller and Better. Will That Mean Cuts to Faculty and Financial Aid?," *Washington Post*, September 13, 2019, https://www.washingtonpost.com/local/education/gwu-aims-to-get-smaller-and-better-will-that-mean-cuts-to-faculty-and-financial-aid/2019/09/12/897ac914-cffe-11e9-b29b-a528dc82154a_story.html; Shannon Mallard, "LeBlanc Aims to Reduce Undergraduate Population by 20 Percent over Five Years," *GW Hatchet*, July 9, 2019, https://www.gwhatchet.com/2019/07/09/leblanc-aims-to-reduce-undergraduate-population-by-20-percent-over-five-years.

18. "Innovation and Justice: Reinventing Selective Colleges," Making Caring Common Project, Harvard Graduate School of Education, April 2021, https://mcc.gse.harvard.edu/reports/innovation-and-justice.

19. Jeffrey J. Selingo, "Harvard and Its Peers Should Be Embarrassed about How Few Students They Educate," *Washington Post*, April 8, 2021, https://www.washingtonpost.com/outlook/harvard-and-its-peers-should-be-embarrassed-about-how-few-students-they-educate/2021/04/08/3c0be99c-97cb-11eb-b28d-bfa7bb5cb2a5_story.html.

20. Daniel Markovits, "How College Became a Ruthless Competition Divorced from Learning," *The Atlantic*, May 6, 2021, https://www.theatlantic.com/ideas/archive/2021/05/marriage-college-status-meritocracy/618795.

21. David L. Kirp, "Why Stanford Should Clone Itself," *New York Times*, April 6, 2021, https://www.nytimes.com/2021/04/06/opinion/stanford-admissions-campus.html.

22. Only a handful of schools reduced tuition for the remote learning delivered during COVID, and in most cases, it was only by 10 percent. See, for example, Emma Kerr and Sarah Wood, "These Colleges Are Giving Tuition Discounts," *U.S. News & World Report*, January 5, 2022, https://www.usnews.com/education/best-colleges/paying-for -college/articles/these-colleges-are-giving-tuition-discounts-this-fall.

23. Kirp, "Why Stanford Should Clone Itself."

24. "Top 100—Lowest Acceptance Rates."

25. Selingo, "Harvard and Its Peers Should Be Embarrassed about How Few Students They Educate."

Chapter 4

1. Benjamin S. Bloom, "Learning for Mastery. Instruction and Curriculum. Regional Education Laboratory for the Carolinas and Virginia, Topical Papers and Reprints, Number 1," *Evaluation Comment* 1, no. 2 (1968): n2.

2. Adapted from James H. Block, "Introduction to *Mastery Learning: Theory and Practice*," in *Mastery Learning: Theory and Practice*, ed. James H. Block (New York: Holt, Rinehart and Winston, 1971), 6–7; and Benjamin S. Bloom, "The 2 Sigma Problem: The Search for Methods of Group Instruction as Effective as One-to-One Tutoring," *Educational Researcher* 13, no. 6 (1984): 4–16.

3. Adam Grant, "Why We Should Stop Grading Students on a Curve," *New York Times*, September 10, 2016, https://www.nytimes .com/2016/09/11/opinion/sunday/why-we-should-stop-grading -students-on-a-curve.html.

4. Jane Swift, "Reason Gazillion We Don't Have More Stem Grads? . . ." Twitter, April 5, 2021, https://twitter.com/janemswift/status /1379117117371518980.

5. Bloom, "Learning for Mastery," 3.

6. Bloom, "The 2 Sigma Problem."

7. Aradhna Krishna and A. Yeşim Orhun, "Gender (Still) Matters in Business School," *Journal of Marketing Research* 59, no. 1 (September 2021): 191–210.

8. Scott E. Carrell, Marianne E. Page, and James E. West, "Sex and Science: How Professor Gender Perpetuates the Gender Gap," *Quarterly Journal of Economics* 125, no. 3 (2010): 1101–1144.

9. Robert W. Fairlie, Florian Hoffmann, and Philip Oreopoulos, "A Community College Instructor like Me: Race and Ethnicity Interactions in the Classroom," *American Economic Review* 104, no. 8 (January 2014): 2567–2591.

10. Steven D. Levitt and Stephen J. Dubner, *Freakonomics: A Rogue Economist Explores the Hidden Side of Everything* (New York: Harper, 2005).

11. Steven Levitt, "Steven Levitt on Freakonomics and the State of Economics," interview with Russ Roberts, *Econlib*, November 9, 2020, https://www.econtalk.org/steven-levitt-on-freakonomics-and-the -state-of-economics, starting at 29:25.

Chapter 5

1. Miramax, "Good Will Hunting | 'My Boy's Wicked Smart' (HD)— Matt Damon, Ben Affleck | Miramax," YouTube, February 26, 2015, https://www.youtube.com/watch?v=hIdsjNGCGz4.

2. Royal Swedish Academy of Sciences, press release, The Nobel Prize, October 10, 2001, https://www.nobelprize.org/prizes/economic-sci ences/2001/press-release.

3. Royal Swedish Academy of Sciences, "A. Michael Spence Facts," The Nobel Prize, accessed September 6, 2022, https://www.nobelprize .org/prizes/economic-sciences/2001/spence/facts.

4. Michael Spence, "Job Market Signaling," *Quarterly Journal of Economics* 87, no. 3 (1973): 355.

5. Lisa Eadicicco, "Apple CEO Tim Cook Explains Why You Don't Need a College Degree to Be Successful," *Business Insider*, March 7,

2019, https://www.businessinsider.com/apple-ceo-tim-cook-why-college
-degree-isnt-necessary-2019-3.

6. Aaron Pressman, "Companies Need to Emphasize Skills over
Degrees, IBM Chair Ginni Rometty Says," *Fortune*, October 1, 2020,
https://fortune.com/2020/10/01/ginni-rometty-ibm-mpw-summit
-skills-diverse-workforce, at 0:03.

7. "Help Wanted: Projecting Jobs and Education Requirements
through 2018," Georgetown Center on Education and the Workforce,
May 7, 2020, https://cew.georgetown.edu/cew-reports/help-wanted.

8. "Recovery: Job Growth and Education Requirements through
2020," Georgetown Center on Education and the Workforce, August
13, 2021, https://cew.georgetown.edu/cew-reports/recovery-job-growth
-and-education-requirements-through-2020.

9. "Moving the Goalposts: How Demand for a Bachelor's Degree Is
Reshaping the Workforce," Burning Glass Technologies, September
2014, https://www.burning-glass.com/wp-content/uploads/Moving_the
_Goalposts.pdf.

10. Catherine Rampell, "Degree Inflation? Jobs That Newly Require
B.A.'s," *New York Times*, December 4, 2012, https://economix.blogs
.nytimes.com/2012/12/04/degree-inflation-jobs-that-newly-require
-b-a-s.

11. Catherine Rampell, "It Takes a B.A. to Find a Job as a File Clerk,"
New York Times, February 19, 2013, https://www.nytimes.com/2013
/02/20/business/college-degree-required-by-increasing-number-of
-companies.html.

12. Frederick M. Hess and Grant Addison, "When College Degrees
Impede Opportunity," *Inside Higher Ed*, December 10, 2018, https://
www.insidehighered.com/views/2018/12/10/essay-how-employers
-college-degree-requirements-can-harm-students.

13. Scott Carlson, "Why the College Degree Is a Signal—and Why
That Should Worry You," *Chronicle of Higher Education*, March 19,
2019, https://www.chronicle.com/newsletter/the-edge/2019-03-19.

14. Khadeeja Safdar, "CEOS Pledge One Million Jobs for Black Americans," *Wall Street Journal*, December 10, 2020, https://www.wsj.com/articles/ceos-pledge-one-million-jobs-for-black-americans-1160760
1610.

15. Aaron Pressman, "Companies Need to Emphasize Skills over Degrees, IBM Chair Ginni Rometty Says," *Fortune*, October 1, 2020, https://fortune.com/2020/10/01/ginni-rometty-ibm-mpw-summit
-skills-diverse-workforce.

16. Nickle LaMoreaux, "Why IBM Chooses Skills over Degrees," Gallup, November 20, 2021, https://www.gallup.com/workplace
/344621/why-ibm-chooses-skills-degrees.aspx.

17. Joseph B. Fuller and Manjari Raman, "Dismissed by Degrees: How Degree Inflation Is Undermining U.S. Competitiveness and Hurting America's Middle Class," Accenture, Grads of Life, and Harvard Business School, October 2017, https://www.hbs.edu/managing-the
-future-of-work/Documents/dismissed-by-degrees.pdf.

18. Lauren A. Rivera, *Pedigree: How Elite Students Get Elite Jobs* (Princeton, NJ: Princeton University Press, 2016), 35.

19. Rivera, *Pedigree*, 29.

20. Vasyl Taras, Marjaana Gunkel, Alexander Assouad, Ernesto Tavoletti, Justin Kraemer, Alfredo Jiménez, Anna Svirina, Weng Si Lei, and Grishma Shah, "The Predictive Power of University Pedigree on the Graduate's Performance in Global Virtual Teams," *European Journal of International Management* 16, no. 4 (2021): 555.

21. Rivera, *Pedigree*, 37.

22. Lauren Rivera, "Firms Are Wasting Millions Recruiting on Only a Few Campuses," *Harvard Business Review*, October 23, 2015, https://
hbr.org/2015/10/firms-are-wasting-millions-recruiting-on-only-a-few
-campuses.

23. Adam Bryant, "In Head-Hunting, Big Data May Not Be Such a Big Deal," *New York Times*, June 20, 2013, https://www.nytimes.com
/2013/06/20/business/in-head-hunting-big-data-may-not-be-such-a
-big-deal.html. Academic researchers have similarly found that

college GPA are not predictive of career success. See, for example, Peter Cappelli, "College, Students, and the Workplace: Assessing Performance to Improve the Fit," *Change: The Magazine of Higher Learning* 24, no. 6 (1992): 55–61; Lauren A. Rivera, "Hiring as Cultural Matching," *American Sociological Review* 77, no. 6 (2012): 999–1022; Lauren A. Rivera, "Ivies, Extracurriculars, and Exclusion: Elite Employers' Use of Educational Credentials," *Research in Social Stratification and Mobility* 29, no. 1 (2011): 71–90.

Chapter 6

1. Mark Edmundson, *Why Teach? In Defense of a Real Education* (New York: Bloomsbury, 2014), xiv–xvi.

2. Michael D. Smith and Rahul Telang, *Streaming, Sharing, Stealing: Big Data and the Future of Entertainment* (Cambridge, MA: MIT Press, 2016).

3. News Corporation (NWSA), "Twenty-First Century Fox, Inc.—Analyst/Investor Day," Yahoo! Finance, August 8, 2013, https://finance.yahoo.com/news/twenty-first-century-fox-inc-220000785.html.

4. Jason Guerrasio, "A Top TV Producer Says Amazon's TV Division Is 'in Way over Their Heads,'" *Business Insider*, October 6, 2017, https://www.businessinsider.com/top-tv-producer-calls-working-with-amazon-a-bit-of-a-gong-show-2017-10.

5. Michael D. Smith and Rahul Telang, *Streaming, Sharing, Stealing: Big Data and the Future of Entertainment* (Cambridge, MA: MIT Press, 2017), 50.

6. Meg James, "Fox's Chase Carey Calls a la Carte Programming 'a Fantasy,'" *Los Angeles Times*, August 8, 2013, https://www.latimes.com/entertainment/envelope/cotown/la-et-ct-foxs-chase-carey-calls-ala-carte-a-fantasy-20130808-story.html.

7. And, in the case of Outlier's recent partnership with Golden Gate University, new ways for students to earn their associates degree online. Lindsay Ellis, "Masterclass's Co-Founder Takes on the Community-College Degree," *Wall Street Journal*, September 7, 2022,

https://www.wsj.com/articles/masterclasss-co-founder-takes-on-the
-community-college-degree-11662525503, "Degrees+: Outlier 100%
Online Associate Degrees Built for You," Golden Gate University,
accessed September 30, 2022, https://www.ggu.edu/degrees-and
-courses/degrees-plus/.

8. "IBM New Collar Jobs: Apprenticeship Program," IBM, accessed
September 6, 2022, https://www.ibm.com/us-en/employment/new
collar/apprenticeships.

9. "Grow with Google Career Certificates," Grow Google, accessed
September 6, 2022, https://grow.google/certificates.

10. Amazon Staff, "Amazon Helps Employees Become Software Engi-
neers in 9 Months," About Amazon, April 13, 2021, https://www
.aboutamazon.com/news/workplace/amazon-helps-employees
-become-software-engineers-in-9-months.

11. Jon Marcus, "MOOCs Keep Getting Bigger. But Do They Work?,"
The Hechinger Report, September 12, 2013, https://hechingerreport
.org/moocs-keep-getting-bigger-but-do-they-work.

12. "COVID Protocols and Reports," Eckerd College, accessed September 6, 2022, https://www.eckerd.edu/coronavirus.

Chapter 7

1. Gabriel Kahn, "The Amazon of Higher Education," Slate, January 2, 2014, accessed September 12, 2022, https://slate.com/human
-interest/2014/01/southern-new-hampshire-university-how-paul
-leblancs-tiny-school-has-become-a-giant-of-higher-education.html.

2. Southern New Hampshire University (SNHU), "Stand Up: Set Your
Own Course at SNHU (:30)," YouTube, December 11, 2017, https://
www.youtube.com/watch?v=sfHYnKMVrfw.

3. Kahn, "The Amazon of Higher Education."

4. Susan Adams, "Meet the English Professor Creating the Billion-
Dollar College of the Future," *Forbes*, March 28, 2019, https://www

.forbes.com/sites/susanadams/2019/03/28/meet-the-english-professor-creating-the-billion-dollar-college-of-the-future/?sh=14aaac7c426b.

5. Lee Gardner, "Mega-Universities Are on the Rise. They Could Reshape Higher Ed as We Know It," *Chronicle of Higher Education*, February 17, 2019, https://www.chronicle.com/article/the-rise-of-the-mega-university.

6. Kahn, "The Amazon of Higher Education."

7. National Center for Education Statistics, "Table 330.10. Average Undergraduate Tuition, Fees, Room, and Board Rates Charged for Full-Time Students in Degree-Granting Postsecondary Institutions, by Level and Control of Institution: 1963–64 through 2020–21," Digest of Education Statistics, accessed September 12, 2022, https://nces.ed.gov/programs/digest/d21/tables/dt21_330.10.asp.

8. Siobhan Lopez, "SNHU Celebrates a Decade without Raising Tuition," press release, Southern New Hampshire University, July 12, 2021, https://www.snhu.edu/about-us/newsroom/press-releases/snhu-celebrates-a-decade-without-raising-tuition.

9. Adams, "Meet the English Professor Creating the Billion-Dollar College of the Future."

10. "SNHU Freezes Tuition at $30,800 for 2018–19," Associated Press, December 10, 2017, https://apnews.com/article/6e203896c37a406d8374f5489436daf0.

11. Natalie Schwartz, "Southern New Hampshire Sets Annual Tuition at $10K and $15K for in-Person Degrees," Higher Ed Dive, December 16, 2020, https://www.highereddive.com/news/southern-new-hampshire-sets-annual-tuition-at-10k-and-15k-for-in-person-d/592310.

12. Adams, "Meet the English Professor Creating the Billion-Dollar College of the Future."

13. Siobhan Lopez, "SNHU Once Again Recognized as a Top Employer in Higher Education, Most Innovative in the North," press release, Southern New Hampshire University, September 13, 2021,

https://www.snhu.edu/about-us/newsroom/press-releases/snhu-once
-again-recognized-as-a-top-employer-in-higher-education.

14. Gardner, "Mega-Universities Are on the Rise."

15. Jamie Beckett, "Stanford Engineering Professors Are Reinventing Online Education with Free Computer Science Courses That Employ New Teaching Technology," Stanford News Service, August 16, 2011, https://news.stanford.edu/pr/2011/pr-compsci-online-o81611.html.

16. Laura McKenna, "The Big Idea That Can Revolutionize Higher Education: 'MOOC,'" *The Atlantic*, May 11, 2012, https://www .theatlantic.com/business/archive/2012/05/the-big-idea-that-can -revolutionize-higher-education-mooc/256926; Andrew Ng and Jennifer Widom, "Origins of the Modern MOOC," Computer Science Department, Stanford University, 2014, http://www.robotics.stanford .edu/~ang/papers/mooc14-OriginsOfModernMOOC.pdf.

17. Larry Hardesty, "Lessons Learned from MITx's Prototype Course," press release, MIT News on Campus and around the World, Massachusetts Institute of Technology, July 16, 2012, https://news .mit.edu/2012/mitx-edx-first-course-recap-0716.

18. iMooX at, "[Emoocs2016] Keynote: Anant Agarwal (CEO edX and Professor MIT)," YouTube, February 23, 2016, https://www .youtube.com/watch?v=NDiH_l9j4ME, at 5:22.

19. TED, "Anant Agarwal: Why Massively Open Online Courses (Still) Matter," YouTube, January 27, 2014, https://www.youtube.com /watch?v=rYwTA5RA9eU, at 3:56.

20. "2021 Impact Report: Serving the World through Learning," Coursera, accessed September 22, 2022, https://about.coursera.org /press/wp-content/uploads/2021/11/2021-Coursera-Impact-Report .pdf; "Coursera's Mission, Vision, and Commitment to Our Community," Coursera, accessed September 12, 2022, https://about.coursera .org; "Exceptional Educators and Partners," Coursera, accessed September 12, 2022, https://www.coursera.org/about/partners; "How Does Coursera Work? Get Started on Coursera," Coursera, accessed September 12, 2022, https://about.coursera.org/how-coursera-works.

21. Gabe Dalporto, "Udacity 2020: The Year in Review," Udacity, January 25, 2021, https://www.udacity.com/blog/2021/01/udacity -2020-the-year-in-review.html.

22. "About Us," edX, accessed September 12, 2022, https://www.edx .org/about-us.

23. Laura Pappano, "The Year of the MOOC," *New York Times*, November 4, 2012, https://www.nytimes.com/2012/11/04/education /edlife/massive-open-online-courses-are-multiplying-at-a-rapid-pace .html.

24. Open edX, "Anant Agarwal, edX—Welcome (10/12/2015)," YouTube, October 21, 2015, https://www.youtube.com/watch?v=lEy TyeNzXDA, at 37:42

25. DardenMBA, "Daphne Koller, Co-Founder of Coursera—February 20, 2013," YouTube, February 21, 2013, https://www.youtube.com /watch?v=Xv1vXiPDlK0, at 20:00.

26. Laura Pappano, "The Boy Genius of Ulan Bator," *New York Times*, September 13, 2013, https://www.nytimes.com/2013/09/15/maga zine/the-boy-genius-of-ulan-bator.html.

27. iMooX at, "[Emoocs2016] Keynote: Anant Agarwal (CEO edX and Professor MIT)," at 7:52.

28. edX team, "Khushbakht Awan," *edX Blog* (blog), September 25, 2013, https://blog.edx.org/khushbakht-awan.

29. Michigan Engineering, "Daphne Koller | The Online Revolution: Learning without Limits," YouTube, February 11, 2014, https://www .youtube.com/watch?v=POJMfQ1N1DI, at 5:30.

30. This approach drew on research showing that immediate retrieval of educational material produced more learning than "elab-orate studying" well after the fact. See Jeffrey D. Karpicke and Janell R. Blunt, "Retrieval Practice Produces More Learning than Elaborative Studying with Concept Mapping," *Science* 331, no. 6018 (November 2011): 772–775; TED, "Daphne Koller: What We're Learning from Online Education," YouTube, August 1, 2012, https://www.youtube .com/watch?v=U6FvJ6jMGHU, at 8:00.

31. TED, "Peter Norvig: The 100,000-Student Classroom," YouTube, June 18, 2012, https://www.youtube.com/watch?v=tYclUdcsdeo, at 2:00.

32. DLDconference, "University 2.0 (Sebastian Thrun, CEO at Udacity) | DLD12," YouTube, January 23, 2012, https://www.youtube.com /watch?v=SkneoNrfadk, at 14:31.

33. iMooX at, "[Emoocs2016] Keynote: Anant Agarwal (CEO edX and Professor MIT)," at 5:23.

34. DLDconference, "University 2.0 (Sebastian Thrun, CEO at Udacity) | DLD12," at 7:40,

35. TED, "Anant Agarwal: Why Massively Open Online Courses (Still) Matter," at 12:11.

36. Michigan Engineering, "Daphne Koller | The Online Revolution: Learning without Limits," at 20:10.

37. "An Introduction to Interactive Programming in Python (Part 1)," Coursera, accessed September 12, 2022, https://www.coursera .org/learn/interactive-python-1.

38. Michigan Engineering, "Daphne Koller | The Online Revolution: Learning without Limits," at 22:50.

39. Chris Piech, Jonathan Huang, Zhenghao Chen, Chuong Do, Andrew Ng, and Daphne Koller, "Tuned Models of Peer Assessment in Moocs," Stanford University, accessed September 12, 2022, https:// www.web.stanford.edu/~cpiech/bio/papers/tuningPeerGrading.pdf.

40. Tamar Lewin, "College of Future Could Be Come One, Come All," *New York Times*, November 21, 2012, https://www.nytimes.com /2012/11/20/education/colleges-turn-to-crowd-sourcing-courses.html; and Michigan Engineering, "Daphne Koller | The Online Revolution: Learning Without Limits," at 27:25.

41. Michigan Engineering, "Daphne Koller | The Online Revolution: Learning without Limits," at 26:30.

42. Khosrow Ghadiri, Mohammad H. Qayoumi, Ellen Junn, and Ping Hsu, "The Transformative Potential of Blended Learning Using MIT

edX's 6.002x Online MOOC Content Combined with Student Team-Based Learning in Class," accessed September 12, 2022, https://images .ctfassets.net/ii9ehdcj88bc/40sNOzvhlP4uIVe8DEHrrF/e5da38375 d9839499a129f2206cd8f29/ed-tech-paper.pdf.

43. ColumbiaLearn, "Conversation | Anant Agarwal—Reinventing Education," YouTube, March 14, 2014, https://www.youtube.com /watch?v=GGu74X3HGzY, at 36:13.

44. Jeffrey R. Young, "From Self-Flying Helicopters to Classrooms of the Future," *Chronicle of Higher Education*, October 1, 2012, https:// www.chronicle.com/article/from-self-flying-helicopters-to-class rooms-of-the-future.

45. "Battushig Myanganbayar," LinkedIn, accessed September 22, 2022, https://www.linkedin.com/in/battushig-myanganbayar-0228b6a2.

46. Woodie Flowers, "New Media's Impact on Education Strategies," EDUCAUSE, January 1, 2001, https://library.educause.edu/resources /2001/1/new-medias-impact-on-education-strategies, p.110.

47. Abigail Johnson Hess, "Here's What Biden's Free Community College Plan Would Cost—and What It Would Save Students," CNBC Make It, July 22, 2021, https://www.cnbc.com/2021/07/22/what-bidens -free-community-college-plan-would-cost-and-save-americans.html.

48. Hess, "Here's What Biden's Free Community College Plan Would Cost."

49. Aaron Rasmussen, "Community College Is the Smart Choice," *Wall Street Journal*, July 15, 2021, https://www.wsj.com/articles/com munity-college-tuition-cost-student-debt-11626379442.

50. Doug Lederman, "Online Education Start-Up, Backed by Research University Credit," *Inside Higher Ed*, August 21, 2019, https://www.insidehighered.com/digital-learning/article/2019/08 /21/new-online-ed-start-aims-community-college-market-university.

51. Woodie Flowers, "Teach Talk: A Contrarian View of MITx: What Are We Doing!?," *MIT Faculty Newsletter* 24, no. 3 (January–February 2012), http://web.mit.edu/fnl/volume/243/flowers.html.

52. Lederman, "Online Education Start-Up."

53. "Tuition and Fees," University of Pittsburgh School of Education, accessed September 12, 2022, https://www.education.pitt.edu /admissions/tuition-and-fees.

54. Callie Burgan, "Pitt-Johnstown Leaders Support Private Vendor's Online Course Offerings," *Tribune-Democrat*, February 27, 2021, https://www.tribdem.com/news/pitt-johnstown-leaders-support -private . . . course-offerings/article_899e1b26-78a4-11eb-b604-8f 5936ae895c.html.

55. National Center for Education Statistics, "Table 315.20. Full-Time Faculty in Degree-Granting Postsecondary Institutions, by Race/Ethnicity, Sex, and Academic Rank: Fall 2015, Fall 2017, and Fall 2018," Digest of Education Statistics, accessed September 12, 2022, https:// nces.ed.gov/programs/digest/d19/tables/dt19_315.20.asp.

56. Amanda Morris and Emily Anthes, "For Some College Students, Remote Learning Is a Game Changer," *New York Times*, August 26, 2021, https://www.nytimes.com/2021/08/23/health/covid-college -disabilities-students.html.

57. David Brooks, "The Campus Tsunami," *New York Times*, May 3, 2012, https://www.nytimes.com/2012/05/04/opinion/brooks-the -campus-tsunami.html.

58. William J. Bennett, "Is Sebastian Thrun's Udacity the Future of Higher Education?," CNN, July 5, 2012, https://www.cnn.com/2012 /07/05/opinion/bennett-udacity-education/index.html.

59. Pappano, "The Year of the MOOC."

60. See "Innovation + Disruption Symposium," Colgate University, May 5, 2014, Vimeo Livestream, accessed September 12, 2022, https:// livestream.com/accounts/4963736/events/2850756/videos/5007203 at the 46:06 mark.

Chapter 8

1. David M. Perry, "Faculty Members Are Not Cashiers," *Chronicle of Higher*, March 17, 2014, https://www.chronicle.com/article/faculty -members-are-not-cashiers.

2. Lisa Bannon and Rebecca Smith, "That Fancy University Course? It Might Actually Come from an Education Company," *Wall Street Journal*, July 6, 2022, https://www.wsj.com/articles/that-fancy-university-course-it-might-actually-come-from-an-education-company-11657126489.

3. Te-Ping Chen and Melissa Korn, "American Colleges Pay Agents to Woo Foreigners, Despite Fraud Risk," *Wall Street Journal*, September 30, 2015, https://www.wsj.com/articles/american-colleges-pay-agents-to-woo-foreigners-despite-fraud-risk-1443665884.

4. Melissa Korn, "Justice Department Urges Judge Not to Dismiss College Financial Aid Antitrust Case," *Wall Street Journal*, July 7, 2022, https://www.wsj.com/articles/justice-department-urges-judge-not-to-dismiss-college-financial-aid-antitrust-case-11657237002.

5. Jeffrey R. Young, "Is There Still a Meaningful Difference between for-Profit and Public Higher Ed?" EdSurge, May 30, 2019, https://www.edsurge.com/news/2019-05-30-is-there-still-a-meaningful-difference-between-for-profit-and-public-higher-ed.

6. Joseph L. Bower and Clayton M. Christensen, "Disruptive Technologies: Catching the Wave," *Harvard Business Review*, January–February 1995, 43–53.

7. Consider Andrew A. King and Baljir Baatartogtokh, "How Useful Is the Theory of Disruptive Innovation?," *MIT Sloan Management Review*, September 15, 2015, https://sloanreview.mit.edu/article/how-useful-is-the-theory-of-disruptive-innovation, where the authors surveyed seventy-seven disruptive innovations and found that only nine fit the characteristics of Christensen's theory.

8. Jena Mcgregor, "Clayton Christensen's Innovation Brain," *Bloomberg*, June 18, 2007, https://www.bloomberg.com/news/articles/2007-06-15/clayton-christensens-innovation-brainbusinessweek-business-news-stock-market-and-financial-advice.

9. Clayton M. Christensen, Michael E. Raynor, and Rory McDonald, "What Is Disruptive Innovation?," *Harvard Business Review*, December 2015, https://hbr.org/2015/12/what-is-disruptive-innovation.

10. "Tesla's Not as Disruptive as You Might Think," *Harvard Business Review*, May 2015, https://hbr.org/2015/05/teslas-not-as-disruptive-as-you-might-think.

11. Joshua Gans, "The Other Disruption: When Innovations Threaten the Organizational Model," *Harvard Business Review*, March 2016, https://hbr.org/2016/03/the-other-disruption.

12. Steve Denning, "Why Clayton Christensen Worries about Apple," *Forbes Magazine*, May 7, 2012, https://www.forbes.com/sites/stevedenning/2012/05/07/why-clayton-christensen-worries-about-apple.

13. See, for example, Shane Greenstein, "The Reference Wars: Encyclopedia Britannica's Decline and Encarta's Emergence," *Strategic Management Journal* 38, no. 5 (March 2016): 995–1017.

14. Jay Greene, "The Inside Story of How Microsoft Killed Its Courier Tablet," CNET, November 1, 2011, https://www.cnet.com/tech/tech-industry/the-inside-story-of-how-microsoft-killed-its-courier-tablet.

15. Mike Colias, "Ford Creates Separate EV, Gas-Engine Divisions in Major Overhaul," *Wall Street Journal*, March 2, 2022, https://www.wsj.com/articles/ford-creates-electric-vehicle-gas-engine-divisions-in-company-reshape-11646222458; William Boston and Georgi Kantchev, "VW Board Ousts CEO Herbert Diess after Pivot to Electric Vehicles," *Wall Street Journal*, July 22, 2022, https://www.wsj.com/articles/volkswagen-ceo-herbert-diess-is-stepping-down-11658507894.

16. Justin Reich, *Failure to Disrupt: Why Technology Alone Can't Transform Education* (Cambridge, MA: Harvard University Press, 2020).

17. Jill Lepore, "What the Gospel of Innovation Gets Wrong," *New Yorker*, June 16, 2014, https://www.newyorker.com/magazine/2014/06/23/the-disruption-machine.

18. Michael Lanford and William G. Tierney, *Creating a Culture of Mindful Innovation in Higher Education* (Albany: State University of New York Press, 2022), 71.

Chapter 9

1. For a more detailed discussion of scale-advantages in the context of digital goods, see Yannis Bakos and Erik Brynjolfsson's excellent articles "Bundling Information Goods: Pricing, Profits, and Efficiency," *Management Science* 45, no. 12 (1999): 1613–1630, and "Bundling and Competition on the Internet" *Marketing Science* 19, no. 1 (2000): 63–82.

2. Michael D. Smith and Rahul Telang, *Streaming, Sharing, Stealing: Big Data and the Future of Entertainment* (Cambridge, MA: MIT Press, 2016).

3. Vanessa Fuhrmans and Kathryn DillFollow, "Blue-Collar Workers Make the Leap to Tech Jobs, No College Degree Necessary," *Wall Street Journal*, April 26, 2022, https://www.wsj.com/articles/tech-jobs-no-college-degree-necessary-11649371535.

4. Amanda Cage, "The Future of the American Labor Market," presented at the Future of Education webinar, hosted by the *Wall Street Journal*, https://www.wsj.com/video/events/amanda-cage-on-the-future-of-the-american-labor-market/D121E642-9678-42FC-8AB3-6E04F3D9853C.html, at 15:01.

5. Joseph Fuller, Christina Langer, and Matt Sigelman, "Skills-Based Hiring Is on the Rise," *Harvard Business Review*, February 11, 2022, https://hbr.org/2022/02/skills-based-hiring-is-on-the-rise.

6. "Installation Address by Lawrence S. Bacow," Harvard University Office of the President, October 5, 2018, https://www.harvard.edu/president/speeches/2018/installation-address-by-lawrence-s-bacow.

7. Brandon Busteed, "Higher Education's Work Preparation Paradox," Gallup, February 25, 2014, https://news.gallup.com/opinion/gallup/173249/higher-education-work-preparation-paradox.aspx.

Chapter 10

1. See, for example, Brett Hollenbeck, "Online Reputation Mechanisms and the Decreasing Value of Chain Affiliation," *Journal of Marketing Research* 55, no. 5 (2018): 636–654.

2. Tom Simonite, "Solve These Tough Data Problems and Watch Job Offers Roll In," *Wired*, October 28, 2017, https://www.wired .com/story/solve-these-tough-data-problems-and-watch-job-offers -roll-in.

3. "Zillow Prize: Zillow's Home Value Prediction (Zestimate)," Kaggle, accessed September 10, 2022, https://www.kaggle.com/c/zillow-prize-1.

4. "Passenger Screening Algorithm Challenge," Kaggle, accessed September 10, 2022, https://www.kaggle.com/c/passenger-screening -algorithm-challenge.

5. "Deep Learning Engineer / Researcher," LinkedIn, accessed September 10, 2022, https://www.linkedin.com/jobs/view/453202560.

6. Adam Bryant, "In Head-Hunting, Big Data May Not Be Such a Big Deal," *New York Times*, June 19, 2013, https://www.nytimes.com /2013/06/20/business/in-head-hunting-big-data-may-not-be-such-a -big-deal.html.

7. Global Silicon Valley, "CEO Jeff Weiner 'All Roads Lead to Linkedin' | ASU GSV Summit," YouTube, May 19, 2017, https://www .youtube.com/watch?v=DKW7dHl3yo0, starting at 14:10.

8. Sean Gallagher and Holly Zanville, "More Employers Are Awarding Credentials: Is a Parallel Higher Education System Emerging?," EdSurge, March 25, 2021, https://www.edsurge.com/news/2021-03-25 -more-employers-are-awarding-credentials-is-a-parallel-higher-educa tion-system-emerging.

9. Paul Fain, "Employers as Educators," *Inside Higher Ed*, July 17, 2019, https://www.insidehighered.com/digital-learning/article/2019 /07/17/amazon-google-and-other-tech-companies-expand-their.

10. "Amazon Pledges to Upskill 100,000 U.S. Employees for in-Demand Jobs by 2025," Amazon, July 11, 2019, https://press.about amazon.com/2019/7/amazon-pledges-to-upskill-100-000-u-s-em ployees-for-in-demand-jobs-by-2025.

11. Kent Walker, "A Digital Jobs Program to Help America's Economic Recovery," Google, July 13, 2020, https://blog.google/outreach

-initiatives/grow-with-google/digital-jobs-program-help-americas
-economic-recovery.

12. Gallup CHRO Conversations, "Why IBM Chooses Skills over Degrees," Gallup, April 13, 2021, https://www.gallup.com/workplace/344621/why-ibm-chooses-skills-degrees.aspx.

13. Monica Nickelsburg, "Microsoft Unveils Sweeping Job Training Initiative to Teach Digital Skills to 25m Impacted by Pandemic," GeekWire, June 30, 2020, https://www.geekwire.com/2020/microsoft-unveils-sweeping-job-training-initiative-teach-digital-skills-25m-impacted-pandemic.

14. Danny Wong, "Sales Reps in Training: An Inside Look at SAP Academy," *HuffPost*, May 3, 2016, https://www.huffpost.com/entry/sales-reps-in-training-an-inside-look-at-sap-academy_b_5715e332e4b0ef1fe48862d9.

15. Valerie Bolden-Barrett, "JPMorgan Chase Commits $350m to Training, Says Degrees Are Not the Future of Work," HR Dive, March 20, 2019, https://www.hrdive.com/news/jpmorgan-chase-commits-350m-to-training-says-degrees-are-not-the-future-o/550825.

16. Daniel McCoy, "Koch Industries Using AI to Find Technology Talent It Can Train," *Wichita Business Journal*, September 14, 2020, https://www.bizjournals.com/wichita/news/2020/09/14/koch-using-ai-to-find-technology-talent.html; Riia O'Donnell, "Case Study: Frito-Lay Whets Students' Appetites for Manufacturing Jobs," HR Dive, September 27, 2019, https://www.hrdive.com/news/case-study-frito-lay-whets-students-appetites-for-manufacturing-jobs/562844.

17. Fain, "Employers as Educators."

18. Douglas Belkin, "Is This the End of College as We Know It?," *Wall Street Journal*, November 12, 2020, https://www.wsj.com/articles/is-this-the-end-of-college-as-we-know-it-11605196909.

19. John Hollis, "Get Your Head in the Cloud: GMU, Nova, & AWS Partner to Create New Degree," *Inside NoVa*, November 8, 2019, https://www.insidenova.com/business_voice/get-your-head-in-the

-cloud-gmu-nova-aws-partner/article_ab34053c-0241-11ea-bdde-876
03c465fa7.html.

20. Lilah Burke, "Community College, with Google as Instructor,"
Inside Higher Ed, October 15, 2019, https://www.insidehighered.com
/digital-learning/article/2019/10/15/google-expands-it-certificate
-program-100-community-colleges.

21. Jeffrey R. Brown, "It's Time to Transform Higher Education,"
University of Illinois, white paper, January 24, 2022, https://uofi.app
.box.com/s/djj98pacghpsikkuqi20cslrjgdij2gm.

22. D. Shapiro, M. Ryu, F. Luie, Q. Liu, and Y. Zhang, "Completing
College 2019 National Report," Signature Report 18, National Student Clearinghouse Research Center, December 2019, https://nscre
searchcenter.org/wp-content/uploads/Completions_Report_2019.pdf.

23. D. Shapiro, M. Ryu, F. Luie, and Q. Liu, "Some College, No Degree:
A 2019 Snapshot for the Nation and 50 States," Signature Report 17,
National Student Clearinghouse Research Center, October 2019, https://
nscresearchcenter.org/wp-content/uploads/SCND_Report_2019.pdf.

24. Jon Marcus, "More Students Are 'Stacking' Credentials En Route
to a Degree," *Wired*, June 2, 2020, https://www.wired.com/story
/students-stacking-credentials-route-degree.

25. Sean R. Gallagher, "Educational Credentials Come of Age: A
Survey on the Use and Value of Educational Credentials in Hiring,"
Center for the Future of Higher Education and Talent Strategy,
Northeastern University, December 2018, https://cps.northeastern
.edu/wp-content/uploads/2021/03/Educational_Credentials_Come_of
_Age_2018.pdf.

26. For example, a 2019 Gallup poll found that between 2013 and
2019, the proportion of US adults who believed college was "very
important" dropped from 70 percent to 51 percent. Among young
adults—who represent the future of higher education—the drop was
even more dramatic, from 74 percent to 41 percent. Stephanie
Marken, "Half in U.S. Now Consider College Education Very Important," Gallup, December 30, 2019, https://www.gallup.com/education
/272228/half-consider-college-education-important.aspx.

Chapter 11

1. Notably, I'm not the only faculty member who felt this way. When I mentioned my experience online to Marsha Lovett, Carnegie Mellon's vice provost for teaching and learning innovation, she responded that "one of the things we learned in the pandemic is that, while it takes effort, in person is not a prerequisite to create community."

2. Bryan Douglas Caplan, *The Case against Education: Why the Education System Is a Waste of Time and Money* (Princeton, NJ: Princeton University Press, 2019), Kindle edition, 50–51.

3. Caplan, *The Case against Education*, 59.

4. Ellen Bara Stolenberg, Melissa C. Aragon, Edgar Romo, Victoria Couch, Destiny McLennan, M. Kevin Eagan, and Nathaniel Kang, "The American Freshman: National Norms Fall 2019," Cooperative Institutional Research Project, Higher Educational Research Institute, Graduate School of Education and Information Studies, University of California at Los Angeles, 2020, https://www.heri.ucla.edu/mono graphs/TheAmericanFreshman2019.pdf, p. 42; Alexander W. Astin, Margo R. King, and Gerald T. Richardson, "The American Freshman: National Norms for Fall 1975," Cooperative Institutional Research Program, American Council on Education, Graduate School of Education, University of California at Los Angeles, 1976, https://www.heri .ucla.edu/PDFs/pubs/TFS/Norms/Monographs/TheAmericanFresh man1975.pdf, p. 18.

5. As an aside, the second most important priority identified in the survey was "making their degrees affordable for everyday people," which 89 percent of the respondents rated as very or somewhat important and 21 percent said should be the single most important priority of universities. Only 2 percent of respondents listed "Supporting the arts and humanities" as the most important priority for universities.

6. Kaustuv Basu, "MOOCs and the Professoriate," *Inside Higher Ed*, May 23, 2012, https://www.insidehighered.com/news/2012/05/23 /faculty-groups-consider-how-respond-moocs.

7. Justin Reich and José A. Ruipérez-Valiente, "The MOOC Pivot," *Science* 363, no. 6423 (November 2019): 130–131.

8. The authors operationalize a country's affluence based on the United Nation's Human Development Index (HDI) and then compare enrollment from students in the 112 countries the UN classifies as high or very high HDI countries versus the thirty-eight countries the UN classifies as low HDI countries.

9. John D. Hansen and Justin Reich, "Democratizing Education? Examining Access and Usage Patterns in Massive Open Online Courses," *Science* 350, no. 6265 (December 4, 2015): 1245–1248.

10. "Economic Diversity and Student Outcomes at Harvard University," The Upshot, *New York Times*, accessed September 11, 2022, https://www.nytimes.com/interactive/projects/college-mobility/harvard-university; "Economic Diversity and Student Outcomes at Massachusetts Institute of Technology," The Upshot, *New York Times*, accessed September 11, 2022, https://www.nytimes.com/interactive/projects/college-mobility/massachusetts-institute-of-technology.

11. The view that online education will exacerbate inequalities is generally referred to in the education literature as the Matthew effect, based on Jesus's parable in Matthew 25:29 that concludes with the statement "everyone who has will be given more" and "whoever does not have, even what he has will be taken from him." Based on what I see in these data, I would gently suggest that my colleagues should pay equal attention to a different parable in Matthew 7:3: "Why do you look at the speck of sawdust in your brother's eye and pay no attention to the plank in your own eye?"

12. Chen Zhenghao, Brandon Alcorn, Gayle Christensen, Nicholas Eriksson, Daphne Koller, and Ezekiel J. Emanuel, "Who's Benefiting from MOOCs, and Why," *Harvard Business Review*, September 22, 2015, https://hbr.org/2015/09/whos-benefiting-from-moocs-and-why.

13. See "Innovation + Disruption Symposium," Colgate University, May 5, 2014, Vimeo Livestream, accessed September 11, 2022, https://livestream.com/accounts/4963736/events/2850756/videos/50072033, at the 1:44:00 mark.

14. Nicholas P. Fandos, "At Meeting, Faculty Question Relationship with Administrators," *Harvard Crimson*, May 8, 2013, https://www.thecrimson.com/article/2013/5/8/faculty-meeting-governance-consultation.

15. Steve Kolowich, "Harvard Professors Call for Greater Oversight of MOOCs," *Chronicle of Higher Education*, May 24, 2013, https://www.chronicle.com/blogs/wiredcampus/harvard-professors-call-for-greater-oversight-of-moocs.

16. Alissa Rothman, "Faculty Vote down Joining edX Pilot Program," *Amherst Student*, April 17, 2013, https://amherststudent.amherst.edu/article/2013/04/17/faculty-vote-down-joining-edx-pilot-program.html.

17. Steve Kolowich, "Why Some Colleges Are Saying No to MOOC Deals, at Least for Now," *Chronicle of Higher Education*, April 29, 2013, https://www.chronicle.com/article/why-some-colleges-are-saying-no-to-mooc-deals-at-least-for-now.

18. Geoffrey Mock, "Faculty Reject Participation in Semester Online Learning Consortium," Duke Today, April 26, 2013, https://today.duke.edu/2013/04/councilvote.

19. "'An Open Letter to Professor Michael Sandel from the Philosophy Department at San Jose State U.,'" *Chronicle of Higher Education*, May 2, 2013, https://www.chronicle.com/article/an-open-letter-to-professor-michael-sandel-from-the-philosophy-department-at-san-jose-state-u.

20. Lee Gardner and Jeffrey R. Young, "California's Move toward MOOCs Sends Shock Waves, but Key Questions Remain Unanswered," *Chronicle of Higher Education*, March 14, 2013, https://www.chronicle.com/article/californias-move-toward-moocs-sends-shock-waves-but-key-questions-remain-unanswered.

21. Lee Gardner, "Survey of California Community Colleges Reveals Drastic Effects of Budget Cuts," *Chronicle of Higher Education*, August 29, 2012, https://www.chronicle.com/article/survey-of-california-community-colleges-reveals-drastic-effects-of-budget-cuts.

22. Pitt News Editorial Board, "Editorial: Online Classes Could Help Make College More Affordable," *Pitt News*, January 8, 2020, https://pittnews.com/article/153698/opinions/editorial-online-classes-could-help-make-college-more-affordable; Bill Schackner, "A NYC Startup and Pitt Extend an Experiment to Cut Intro Course Prices," *Pittsburgh Post-Gazette*, January 7, 2020, https://www.post-gazette.com/news/education/2020/01/07/University-of-Pittsburgh-Outlier-online-education-tuition-price-calculus-psychology-higher-education/stories/202001060116.

23. Pitt Faculty Organizing Committee, "Letter to the Editor: Faculty Organizers Object to Outlier Courses," *University Times*, March 20, 2020, https://www.utimes.pitt.edu/news/letter-editor-faculty.

24. Melinda Ciccocioppo, "Op-Ed: A Word of Caution to Students about Outlier Courses," *Pitt News*, June 16, 2020, https://pittnews.com/article/158385/opinions/op-ed-a-word-of-caution-to-students-about-outlier-courses.

25. Kaustuv Basu, "Faculty Groups Consider How to Respond to MOOCs," *Inside Higher Ed*, May 23, 2012, https://www.insidehighered.com/news/2012/05/23/faculty-groups-consider-how-respond-moocs.

26. Mark Edmundson, "The Trouble with Online Education," *New York Times*, July 19, 2012, https://www.nytimes.com/2012/07/20/opinion/the-trouble-with-online-education.html.

27. Robert Talbert, "The Trouble with Khan Academy," *Chronicle of Higher Education*, July 3, 2012, https://www.chronicle.com/blognetwork/castingoutnines/2012/07/03/the-trouble-with-khan-academy/?cid2=gen_login_refresh&cid=gen_sign_in.

28. Bob Samuels, "Being Present," *Inside Higher Ed*, January 24, 2013, https://www.insidehighered.com/views/2013/01/24/essay-flaws-distance-education#ixzz2IujdcaLm.

29. John Warner, "ASU Is the 'New American University': It's Terrifying," *Inside Higher Ed*, January 25, 2015, https://www.insidehighered.com/blogs/just-visiting/asu-new-american-university-its-terrifying.

30. Joshua Kim, "Alternative Credentials, Scaled Degrees, and the New Higher Ed Matthew Effect," *Inside Higher Ed*, August 10, 2020, https://www.insidehighered.com/blogs/learning-innovation/alternative-credentials-scaled-degrees-and-new-higher-ed-matthew-effect.

31. Leesa Wheelahan and Gavin Moodie, "Gig Qualifications for the Gig Economy: Micro-Credentials and the 'Hungry Mile,'" *Higher Education* 83, no. 6 (March 2021): 1279–1295.

32. "Facts and Figures," Arizona State University, accessed September 22, 2022, https://www.asu.edu/about/facts-and-figures.

33. Outlier.org, "Outlier.org Expands University Partnership Model to Offer Its Courseware Directly to Universities," press release, Cision PR Newswire, August 18, 2020, https://www.prnewswire.com/news-releases/outlierorg-expands-university-partnership-model-to-offer-its-courseware-directly-to-universities-301113964.html.

34. Khosrow Ghadiri, Mohammad H. Qayoumi, Ellen Junn, and Ping Hsu, "The Transformative Potential of Blended Learning Using MIT edX's 6.002x Online MOOC Content Combined with Student Team-Based Learning in Class," *environment* 8, no. 14 (2013): 14–29, accessed September 12, 2022, https://images.ctfassets.net/ii9ehdcj88bc/4OsNOzvhlP4uIVe8DEHrrF/e5da38375d9839499a129f2206cd8f29/ed-tech-paper.pdf.

35. Robert M. Hutchins, "The Threat to American Education," *Colliers Weekly*, December 30, 1944, 20–21, accessed September 20, 2022, https://www.unz.com/print/Colliers-1944dec30-00020.

36. Robert Zemsky, *Checklist for Change: Making American Higher Education a Sustainable Enterprise* (New Brunswick, NJ: Rutgers University Press, 2013), 40. President Conant's concerns were unfounded, as he acknowledged in a 1946 article in *Life* magazine. The article quotes President Conant as calling the servicemen admitted under the GI Bill "the most mature and promising students Harvard has even had." See Charles J. V. Murphy, "GIs at Harvard: They Are the Best Students in College's History," *Life*, July 17, 1946, 16–22. Similarly, a 1947 article in the journal *Educational Outlook* observed that students admitted under the GI Bill were "hogging the honor rolls and

the Dean's lists" and "walking away with the top marks in all of their courses." The article's conclusion? "Far from being an educational problem, the veteran has become an asset to higher education." Benjamin Fine, "Veterans Raise College Standards," *Educational Outlook*, 22 (November 1947), 54.

Chapter 12

1. James Klemaszewski, "ASU Graduating Senior Inspired to Become a Doctor through Son's Illness," ASU News, March 5, 2021, https://news.asu.edu/20210305-asu-graduate-inspired-become-doctor-through-sons-illness.

2. "Battushig Myanganbayar," LinkedIn, accessed September 22, 2022, https://www.linkedin.com/in/battushig-myanganbayar-0228b6a2.

3. Scott Plous, "2013 Day of Compassion Award," Social Psychology Network, 2013, https://www.socialpsychology.org/awards/day-of-compassion/2013.

4. Balesh Jindal, "The Day of Compassion," Social Psychology Network, September 2013, https://www.socialpsychology.org/awards/day-of-compassion/2013/pdf/1-DelhiSchool.pdf.

5. Mark Halberstadt, "Thank You Khan Academy!" YouTube, May 21, 2011, https://www.youtube.com/watch?v=UDA3fF6WsVQ, at 6:10.

6. "C. Mark Halberstadt," LinkedIn, accessed September 30, 2022, https://www.linkedin.com/in/cmarkhalberstadt.

7. Natalie Van Kleef Conley, "From IT Certificate Completers to Googlers," Google, August 10, 2020, https://blog.google/outreach-initiatives/grow-with-google/it-certificate-completers-googlers.

8. "2021 Impact Report: Serving the World through Learning," Coursera, accessed September 22, 2022, https://about.coursera.org/press/wp-content/uploads/2021/11/2021-Coursera-Impact-Report.pdf.

9. "Accelerating Our Movement: 2021 edX Impact Report," edX, 2013, https://assets.ctfassets.net/ii9ehdcj88bc/5xW5SCQ7eYUh8hEY

PEyL4l/4ad615c638f281085af0ce18f59de874/2021-edx-impact
_report-english.pdf.

10. "Fiscal Year 2021 Fall Enrollment Report," Arizona Board of Regents, accessed September 22, 2022, https://www.azregents.edu /sites/default/files/reports/enrollment-report_2021.pdf; "About SNHU," Southern New Hampshire University, accessed September 22, 2022, https://www.snhu.edu/about-us.

11. Nikai Salcido, "ASU Set to Celebrate More than 18,000 Students at Spring Commencement," *ASU News*, May 4, 2022, https://news .asu.edu/20220504-sun-devil-life-asu-spring-2022-commencement -preview; Pamme Boutselis, "Celebrating the Achievements of 23,000 SNHU Graduates Worldwide," Southern New Hampshire University, May 11, 2020, https://www.snhu.edu/about-us/newsroom/commu nity/class-of-2020.

12. National Center for Education Statistics, "Table 311.15. Number and Percentage of Students Enrolled in Degree-Granting Postsecond- ary Institutions, by Distance Education Participation, Location of Student, Level of Enrollment, and Control and Level of Institution: Fall 2019 and Fall 2020," Digest of Education Statistics, accessed September 22, 2022, https://nces.ed.gov/programs/digest/d21/tables /dt21_311.15.asp.

13. Matt Sigelman, "The Emerging Degree Reset," Burning Glass Institute, February 9, 2022, https://www.burningglassinstitute.org /research/the-emerging-degree-reset.

14. William Bunch, *After the Ivory Tower Falls: How College Broke the American Dream and Blew up Our Politics—and How to Fix It* (New York: William Morrow, 2022), Kindle edition, 276.

15. "Vision & Mission" Carnegie Mellon University, accessed Sep- tember 22, 2022, https://www.cmu.edu/about/mission.html.

16. To see what I mean, compare CMU's mission statement to the clarity and specificity of mission statements of top companies like Google ("Our mission is to organize the world's information and make it universally accessible and useful") or even top educational

platforms like Khan Academy ("Our mission is to provide a free, world-class education for anyone, anywhere").

17. Jerry Useem, "Business School, Disrupted," *New York Times*, May 31, 2014, https://www.nytimes.com/2014/06/01/business/business -school-disrupted.html.

18. Consider that in his January 24, 2012, State of the Union address, President Barack Obama said, "it's not enough for [the Federal government] to increase student aid. We can't just keep subsidiz- ing skyrocketing tuition; we'll run out of money. . . . So let me put colleges and universities on notice: If you can't stop tuition from going up, the funding you get from taxpayers will go down." Barack Obama, "Remarks by the President in State of the Union Address," The White House, Office of the Press Secretary, January 24, 2012, https://obamawhitehouse.archives.gov/the-press-office/2012/01/24 /remarks-president-state-union-address.

Index